Praise for *The Darwin Awards: Evolution in Action*

"Hilarious . . . A book often is defined as good by saying you can't put it down. With *Darwin Awards* you can. Then pick it up again. And again." —*The Flint Journal* (Michigan)

"A warning to all dimwits." —Salon.com

"One of the drawbacks to not teaching the theory of evolution in schools is that some people wind up learning the stuff the hard way . . . Darwin-worthy departures are sent in from people all over the world. One lesson is that fatal stupidity knows no boundaries." —*Sarasota Herald-Tribune*

"*The Darwin Awards* is a riot to read. Deeply entertaining." —*San Francisco Weekly*

"D'oh!" —*Creative Loafing* (Atlanta, Georgia)

A graduate of the University of California–Berkeley with a degree in molecular biology, **Wendy Northcutt** began collecting the stories that make up the Darwin Awards in 1993, and founded www.DarwinAwards.com soon thereafter. Her award-winning website is one of the most popular humor pages on the web, and has been profiled in *USA Today*, *The Wall Street Journal*, and *Entertainment Weekly*, and on NPR's *All Things Considered*, among others. Wendy lives in Silicon Valley, California.

Cartoon of Charles Darwin, from the *Vanity Fair* series "Men of the Day," published in 1871.

I love fools' experiments,
I am always making them.
—Charles Darwin (1809–1882)

the darwinĀwards

II

UNNATURAL SELECTION

Wendy Northcutt

A PLUME BOOK

The Darwin Awards II: Unnatural Selection contains cautionary tales of misadventure. It is intended to be viewed as a safety manual, not a how-to guide. The stories illustrate evolution working through natural selection: Those whose actions have lethal personal consequences are weeded out of the gene pool. Your decisions can kill you, so pay attention and stay alive.

For further information about how to avoid the scythe of natural selection, read Darwin's lessons on safety, science, and the social implications of evolution.

Safety class
www.DarwinAwards.com/book/teach.html

PLUME
Published by the Penguin Group
Penguin Putnam Inc., 375 Hudson Street, New York, New York 10014, U.S.A.
Penguin Books Ltd, 80 Strand, London WC2R 0RL, England
Penguin Books Australia Ltd, 250 Camberwell Road, Camberwell, Victoria 3124, Australia
Penguin Books Canada Ltd, 10 Alcorn Avenue, Toronto, Ontario, Canada M4V 3B2
Penguin Books (N.Z.) Ltd, Cnr Rosedale and Airborne Roads, Albany,
Auckland 1310, New Zealand

Penguin Books Ltd, Registered Offices: Harmondsworth, Middlesex, England

Published by Plume, a member of Penguin Putnam Inc. Previously published in a Dutton edition.

First Plume Printing, April 2003

10 9 8 7 6 5 4 3 2 1

The Library of Congress has catalogued the Dutton edition as follows:

Northcutt, Wendy.
The Darwin awards II: unnatural selection / Wendy Northcutt.
p. cm.
Includes index.
ISBN 0-525-94623-3 (hc.)
ISBN 0-452-28401-5 (pbk.)
1. Stupidity—Anecdotes. I. Title.
BF431 .N67 2000
081—dc21
00-059634

Printed in the United States of America
Original hardcover design by Leonard Telesca

To my parents, who appreciate my eccentricities.
To #1 fans Karol, Darrell, and the little K's.
To Ian for your considered opinions.
To Bill & Kelly, blessed with the forest.
To Carol for your infectious exuberance.
To my Philosophy Forum for your passionate convictions.
To editor Mitch Hoffman: patient, persistent, and wise.
To Henry Kaufman for sage legal advice.
And to Jacob.

Contents

Introduction: What Are They?   1

The Darwin Awards need context to be fully appreciated. There are rules, traditions, and procedures to cleave to when awarding the ignominious Darwin Award. Understand the gestalt in this easy-to-remember history.

What Are They?   2
Rules and Eligibility   3
Darwin's Theory of Evolution   6
Surviving Stupidity   8
Where Do Darwins Come From?   9

CHAPTER 1

Penance: Seven Deadly Sins   11

Religions have long waged war against the seven deadly sins. Here's proof that evolution is fighting the same battle. Lust, vanity, gluttony, greed, sloth, envy, and wrath: all are fatal when carried to excess. From sensual skunk play to the vanity of amateur liposuction, indulgence in the deadly vices leads to trouble.

Discussion: Kismet, Karma, Destiny   12
Darwin Award: Vanity: Liposuction Tragedy   14
Darwin Award: Vanity: Perilous Pose   15
Darwin Award: Wrath: Throwing Stones   16
Darwin Award: Greed: Crystal Daze   17
Darwin Award: Sloth: Sleepfalling   18
Darwin Award: Envy: Flames of Passion   19
Darwin Award: Envy: Moscow Marauder   20
Darwin Award: Gluttony: Ethanol Schmethanol   21

Honorable Mention: Gluttony: Men Eating Chili   22
Personal Account: Lust: Emergency Room Excitement   23

CHAPTER 2

Women: Femme Fatalities   25

Women make the world go round, but not the Darwin Awards.
Rarely does the fair sex grace our annals! Here collected read
every story of "Darwinian woman" in the book, fourteen in all.
They comprise a group portrait of Homo sapiens *femme fatal.*

Discussion: Civilization Memes   26
Darwin Award: Fast Food Fatality   29
Darwin Award: Enraged Elephant   30
Darwin Award: Rubbish!   31
Darwin Award: Christmas Tree   32
Darwin Award: Testing Faith   33
Darwin Award: That Sinking Feeling   34
Honorable Mention: Aircraft Airhead   35
Darwin Award: Fatal Footwear Fashion   36
Honorable Mention: Explosive Mix of Girls   37
Honorable Mention: Snow Bunnies   38
Honorable Mention: Dumb Drunk   39
Personal Account: Eat the Young   40
Personal Account: Brush with Stupidity   41

CHAPTER 3

Water: All Washed Up   **43**

*Our bodies are more liquid than solid, yet we have forgotten
a surprising amount about water in our climb out of the
primeval ooze. Here's why you should avoid submerging your
head for prolonged periods.*

Discussion: Weed Seeds and Biodiversity   44
Darwin Award: Fishing with No Compass   46
Darwin Award: Duct Tape   47
Darwin Award: Dodging Drink Dues   48
Darwin Award: Walking on Water   49
Darwin Award: Dive to Death   50
Darwin Award: Passionate Plunge   51
Darwin Award: Show-Off   52
Honorable Mention: All Aboard   53
Honorable Mention: Sewer Shower   54
Urban Legend: Brewery Mishap   55

CHAPTER 4

Technology: Engines of Destruction   **57**

*We evolved from living in trees to living amongst modern
machinery . . . but some men haven't yet made that evolutionary
leap. Here's a primer on the dangers of our own devices.*

Discussion: Car Safety   58
Darwin Award: Do It Yourself, Do Yourself In   61
Darwin Award: Two Avalanche Alaskan   63
Darwin Award: Forklift Safety Video   65
Darwin Award: Electrifying Stunt   66
Darwin Award: Intersecting Darwins   67

Darwin Award: Power Punch Proves Fatal   68
Darwin Award: Scooter Snuff   69
Darwin Award: Circular Reasoning   70
Darwin Award: Sweet Release   71
Darwin Award: Snowball's Chance in Hell   73
Darwin Award: Sand Surfing   74
Honorable Mention: House Hunting Gone Awry   75
Honorable Mention: Coors Light and the UltraLight   76
Urban Legend: Mad Trombonist   77
Personal Account: Robot Reaper   79
Personal Account: Prop Arc Safety   80
Personal Account: Miracle Mile   81

CHAPTER 5

Men: Male-functions   **83**

Men suffer more than most from their own personalities and natural inclinations. Here's hoping the desire to shoot arrows, show off to young women, aim flying kicks, and accept ludicrous dares become a bit less common someday.

Discussion: Online Safety   84
Darwin Award: Rappin' on Heaven's Door   87
Darwin Award: Fantastic Plastic Lover   88
Darwin Award: Bulletproof?   89
Darwin Award: New Dating Technique   90
Darwin Award: God Saves?   91
Darwin Award: Settle the Score   92
Darwin Award: Hardheads   93
Darwin Award: Ur-inate-iot   94
Darwin Award: A Fell Death   95
Honorable Mention: Cheez Whiz   96
Honorable Mention: Trash Compactor   98
Honorable Mention: Archery Practice   99

Honorable Mention: Tied to His Work   100
Honorable Mention: Chicken with a Train   101
Honorable Mention: Toilet Trap   102
Urban Legend: The Bricklayer   103
Personal Account: Tourist Trap   105
Personal Account: Tube Snake   107

CHAPTER 6

Animals: Pall of the Wild   109

The call of the wild is heard less frequently in our tame neighborhoods, but people still manage to get in trouble with sheep, sharks, wasps, and lobsters. Tales of wilderness woe remind us who's really in charge of the earth.

Discussion: Dogs and Darwinism   110
Darwin Award: Hornet Challenge   114
Darwin Award: Fish Gag   115
Darwin Award: Sheep Sleep   116
Honorable Mention: Doggone Foot   117
Urban Legend: Cactus Tales   118
Personal Account: Polar Bear Lesson   121
Personal Account: Feeding the Dolphins   122
Personal Account: Horsing Around   123
Urban Legend: Lobster Vasectomy   124

CHAPTER 7

Explosions: Out with a Bang! 125

Our fascination with incendiary devices is as old as the first blazing firepit. Now that the campfire days are gone, we may eventually lose our love of explosives . . . but we will undoubtedly lose a few limbs in the process.

Discussion: Intelligent Design Theory 126
Darwin Award: Out with a Bang! 129
Darwin Award: Grenade Juggler 131
Darwin Award: Fireworks Fiasco 132
Darwin Award: Shell Shot 133
Darwin Award: Guitars 'n' Guns 134
Honorable Mention: Kaboom! 135
Honorable Mention: Plane Stupid 136
Urban Legend: Fifteen Minutes of Flame 137
Personal Account: A Medieval Tale 139
Personal Account: Workin' on the Railroad 141
Personal Account: Man and Cactus 142
Personal Account: Man with Gas Can 143
Personal Account: Instant Sunrise 145

CHAPTER 8

Outlaws: Crime and Punishment 149

Living outside the law is a time-honored tradition, but an increasingly dangerous profession. College tuition is cheaper and more profitable than the cost these criminals bear to learn that crime does pay — in pain.

Discussion: City Living 150
Darwin Award: Human Popsicle 152

Darwin Award: Ski Theft Backfires   154
Darwin Award: Escaping Conviction   155
Darwin Award: Killing Time   156
Darwin Award: Just Say No!   158
Darwin Award: Stab in the Dark   159
Darwin Award: You Said a Mouthful   160
Honorable Mention: The Sting   161
Honorable Mention: Ferguson 2, Thieves 0   162
Honorable Mention: Morsel of Evidence   163
Honorable Mention: Call Girl   164
Honorable Mention: Bodacious Bud   165
Honorable Mention: Siphon!   166
Honorable Mention: Planning Ahead   167
Honorable Mention: Sobriety Test   168
Personal Account: Medical Misadventures   169

CHAPTER 9

Disqualified: Losing Is Its Own Reward   **173**

Some deaths deserve a Darwin and some don't. Nominees are occasionally disqualified by readers correcting my judgment or knowledge. The following stories are not Darwins. Here's why.

Not a Darwin: Do Bikes Float?   174
Not a Darwin: Underwire Bras Deadly   175
Not a Darwin: Texas A&M Bonfire   176
Not a Darwin: Body Canyoning   178
Not a Darwin: Our Brightest Cheerleaders   180
Not a Darwin: Fatal Case of Hiccups   181
Not a Darwin: Ice Floe Frolic   182
Not a Darwin: Shotgun Pepsi   184
Not a Darwin: Mania Strikes Back   186

CHAPTER 10

Classic Dozen: Better Read than Dead   189

These traditional commemorations of vast stupidity are a must-have in every mental collection. Enjoy re-reading your favorites: the twelve cream of the crop from the twentieth century.

Discussion: Speciation   190
Darwin Award: JATO   193
Darwin Award: Junk Food Junkie   195
Darwin Award: Midnight Special   196
Darwin Award: Wrong Time, Wrong Place   197
Darwin Award: Count Your Chickens   198
Darwin Award: The Last Supper   199
Honorable Mention: Lawnchair Larry   200
Honorable Mention: Revenge of the Gopher   203
Urban Legend: Frog Giggin' Accident   204
Urban Legend: Metallica Concert Misadventure   205
Urban Legend: Scuba Divers and Forest Fires   208
Urban Legend: Dog and Jeep   210

Appendices   213

1. Website Biography   213
2. Author Biography   215
3. Forum Decorum   216
4. Godwin's Law   221

Story Index   222

the
darwin Awards
II

Against stupidity,
the Gods themselves
contend in vain.

—Friedrich von Schiller

Introduction:
What Are They?

A fool and his life are soon parted.

The Darwin Awards need context to be fully appreciated. There are rules, traditions, and procedures to cleave to when awarding the ignominious Darwin Award. Understand the gestalt in this easy-to-remember history.

WHAT ARE THEY?

Darwin Awards commemorate those individuals who ensure the long-term survival of our species by removing themselves from the gene pool in a sublimely idiotic fashion. The stories are true accidental blunders that cost the hapless perpetrator his life. But don't mistake the intent of the humor. We are not poking tasteless fun at accidents. On the contrary!

Darwin Awards poke fun at decisions that were obviously wrong at the time. In doing so, we celebrate examples of natural selection in action. We applaud those individuals who demonstrate the manifest unfitness of their genes by failing Life 101 in the twenty-first century.

The Darwin Awards you are about to read honor the not-so-unexpected demise of men who read fireworks labels using a cigarette lighter. They are for those who eat from a bulging can, stand behind a running automobile, and kiss the contagious mouths of sick grandchildren. Darwin Awards are for people who repeatedly stump us with their cluelessness.

And they are for those of us who somehow survived our own foolish risks. Remember those experiments with matches and plastic bottles, the fraying rope swing over the river, the jerry-built treehouse? Darwin Awards remind us how close we've come to winning an award ourselves.

What *aren't* they?

Darwin Awards do not make fun of people caught in the blind vise of fate. They are not for those struggling to overcome cruel circumstances. They are not for illegal immigrants frozen in airplane landing gear. They are not for poverty-stricken people who steal oil from a broken pipeline to survive—until someone lights a cigarette. Desperate times call for desperate measures, which are often sensible when you consider the bleak alternative.

Rather we honor those who unthinkingly engineer their own downfalls, oblivious to warning signs that the rest of us automatically heed. The chubby man who volunteers for a neighbor's liposuction experiment. The stoned woman who sleeps on a steep roof. The inevitable whack to the head protruding from a car window. Each earns a Darwin for the unsurprisingly deadly outcome of their decision.

RULES AND ELIGIBILITY

To qualify, nominees must improve the gene pool by eliminating themselves from the human race using astonishingly stupid means. Candidates are evaluated using the five rules of death, excellence, veracity, maturity, and self-selection.

The candidate must be eliminated from the gene pool.

This means death or, less commonly, sterilization.

*The candidate must show an astounding
misapplication of common sense.*

Being hit by a falling safe is just bad luck. Pulling a safe
downstairs, on the other hand, particularly while your shoelace
is untied, is blatantly tempting fate—and being squashed by it
is grounds for a Darwin.

The event must be verified.

Reputable newspaper articles, confirmed television reports,
and responsible eyewitnesses are considered valid sources.

The candidate must be capable of sound judgment.

We're not talking about kids who imitate television stunt
men, or adults addled by insulin shock. But if you choose to
become inebriated and impair your own thinking, you can win
a Darwin despite the self-inflicted infirmity.

The candidate must be the cause of his own demise.

One cannot have the greatness of a Darwin Award thrust
upon oneself. Only a person who *voluntarily* throws caution to
the wind, demonstrating his *own* manifest unfitness for survival, is worthy of this honor.

Things that are not a Darwin, but not safe either, include:
• Whizzing on an electric wire (who knew?)
• Smoking in an oxygen tent; being hit by a train or automobile, particularly while talking on a cell phone; and
   most autoerotic deaths (all too common).

- Killing others. The death of an innocent bystander absolutely rules out a Darwin Award. We don't recognize those who take other people out of the gene pool, even if they share some DNA in common.

There are some "rules purists" who insist that those who have already procreated are ineligible for a Darwin Award. This is tenable in theory, as eliminating genes prior to reproduction is most efficient. However it is impractical to determine the reproductive status of every nominee, and the trait may only be lethal in a particular combination of genes. A fascination with fire, for example, isn't dangerous if coupled with a healthy respect for fire. So a parent who possesses a deadly combination can win a Darwin without passing the trait along to his children. For these reasons, the existence of offspring doesn't eliminate a candidate from the running.

This book contains four categories of stories:

- *Darwin Awards* nominees lost their reproductive capacity, generally because they died. This is the only category eligible to compete for the Darwin Award.
- *Honorable Mentions* are foolish misadventures that stop short of the ultimate sacrifice, but still illustrate the innovative spirit of Darwin Award candidates.
- *Urban Legends* are cautionary tales of evolution in action, and are so popular they have become part of the Internet culture. Various versions are widely circulated, but their origins are largely unknown. They should be understood as the fables they are. Any resemblance to actual events, or to persons living or dead, is purely coincidental.

- *Personal Accounts* were submitted by loyal readers blowing the whistle on stupidity, and are plausible but unverified narratives. In some cases readers submitting Personal Accounts have been identified with their permission, but this does not necessarily mean that the sources are directly associated with their Personal Accounts.

Darwin Awards, Honorable Mentions, and Personal Accounts are known or suspected to be true. Look for the words "Confirmed by Darwin" under the title, which generally indicate that a story was backed up by multiple submissions and by more than one reputable media source.

"Unconfirmed by Darwin" indicates fewer credible submissions and the unavailability of direct confirmation of media sources. In "unconfirmed" Darwin Awards or Honorable Mentions, names have often been changed and details of events altered to protect the innocent (and for that matter, the guilty).

DARWIN'S THEORY OF EVOLUTION

In order to appreciate the Darwin Awards, it helps to have a working understanding of natural selection. Evolution occurs through the mechanism of natural selection. Charles Darwin proposed this theory in his book *Origin of Species*, which presented copious evidence that species evolve to fit their environments.

According to Darwin, four elements characterize natural selection:

A species must show variation.

Humans exhibit this quality in abundance. We are taller or shorter, brawnier or bluer or curlier. Numerous differences exist even between identical twins as they too are subject to random genetic mutations caused by chemical and mechanical stresses.

Variations must be inheritable.

Children resemble their parents because we inherit half our genetic complement from each. Even complex characteristics such as personality have strong, heritable genetic components.

Not all individuals survive to reproduce.

A single pair of mice will multiply to one trillion mice in twenty-five generations (about six years) if each pair has six surviving children. But many offspring die without reproducing. Humans also fail to achieve 100 percent survival rates, and are thus susceptible to natural selection.

Some individuals cope with selective pressures better than others.

Due to inherited traits, some animals survive the onslaught of predators and harsh winters better, and thus leave more offspring. Successful traits become more prevalent as generations pass, and, time after time, as those unable to deal effectively with their environment succumb at an earlier age.

The four criteria of variation, heritability, selection, and fitness have been proven to be effective in countless successful

genetic experiments. From the breeding of domestic dogs to the creation of new food crops, and even to mutant viruses in the lab, we hold the tools of evolution in our hands.

The stories in this book vividly illustrate these principles in all their selective glory, from the sublimely ironic to the pathetically stupid. Charles Darwin himself would, we think, be amused by these examples of trial and fatal error.

SURVIVING STUPIDITY

We have all encountered people too stupid to be alive.

I met a woman atop the steep gravel road outside my house. She had taken her trash to the pickup spot, and the lid had blown off into a ravine. It needed to be retrieved. The only problem was that it now lay at the bottom of a cliff.

The woman made brief nervous forays down the incline, pacing to and fro indecisively. Her husband, she said, claimed he'd climbed straight down to grab the lid. She seemed determined to follow in his footsteps, which surely meant a painful fall. I left her hovering on the edge of the cliff, trying to find a safe passage down.

She was a Darwin in the making. I can picture her, scratched and bruised after a tumble into a bramble-infested ravine, saying, "I did it because my husband says he does it!"

We make judgments about risk all the time. Evaluating the distance of a jump, selecting which wire to cut, deciding to walk under a ladder. Common sense guides our choices, sometimes embedded in useful superstitions. It probably *is* bad luck to walk beneath ladders, in the path of falling ladder climbers and their gear, but it might be more dangerous to walk into the street to get around the ladder. The better able we are to assess risk and take preventive measures, the longer we live.

Share your favorite stupidity survival tale!
www.DarwinAwards.com/book/stupidity.html

In September 1996 a man was crushed to death on a stairway at the Sammis Real Estate and Insurance office in Huntington, New York, while he was stealing the office's six hundred pound safe. He violated a cardinal rule to keep in mind while moving heavy objects: never stand between the object and the call of gravity. The safe was empty at the time of the incident.

(Darwin Award nomination of unknown veracity,
culled from a decade of email.)

Where Do Darwins Come From?

Darwin Awards are passed from friend to friend in a perpetuation of one of the first email chain letters. They are binary fossils from the Dawn of the Internet.

Darwin Awards are based on implausible but true news reports. The book also includes magnificently fictitious Urban Legends crafted by anonymous artisans, Honorable Mentions saluting the current stupidity of future Darwin hopefuls, and Personal Accounts of embarrassingly monumental stupidity.

Each story begins with an alert reader who presents a nomination culled from newspaper, TV, or personal experience. An informal worldwide network of correspondents makes sure that few examples of egregious stupidity go unnoticed. I select

the best stories based on their adherence to the rules and spirit of the Darwin Awards, and write them in a jocular vein.

My subjective sense of humor is refined by enthusiastic website readers, who vote on the stories, point out errors, add information, and dispute dubious details. During this process, stories are often modified and occasionally removed from consideration (See the chapter *Losing Is Its Own Reward*, page 173.) Thus the Darwin Awards you will read in this book originate from, and are polished by, attentive readers who care deeply about the outcome of the selection process. The Darwin Awards are "of the people, by the people, and for the people."

Because the outcomes are sometimes tragic, these stories are best read in small doses. The entertainment value springs from the difference between our expectations of how people ought to behave, and the counterproductive manner in which they actually do behave. To best appreciate the humor, focus on the method behind the madness . . . and feel free to laugh at these unfortunates, knowing that a thousand others have laughed before you!

Darwin Awards: Chlorinating the Gene Pool
(Motto suggested by readers to illustrate
the evolutionary spirit shown by our nominees.)

CHAPTER 1

Penance:

Seven Deadly Sins

The tree of life is self-pruning.

Religions have long waged war against the seven deadly sins. Here's proof that evolution is fighting the same battle. Lust, vanity, gluttony, greed, sloth, envy, and wrath: all are fatal when carried to excess. From sensual skunk play to the vanity of amateur liposuction, indulgence in the deadly vices leads to trouble.

DISCUSSION: KISMET, KARMA, DESTINY

Are you superstitious?

We enjoy believing in abstract balancing principles. There ought to be a force that gives each what he's earned, call it kismet, karma, or destiny. And yet we also believe in the opposite—lucky slot machines and winning streaks. Don't you sometimes walk around a ladder, or kiss your exam paper for good luck? Superstitious beliefs are imbedded in our personalities.

The Darwin Awards celebrate another sort of religion—that of final justice according to the divine laws of nature. Darwin winners suffer a practical form of karma. They prove our theory that if you don't use your head to enhance your survival, you'll be fingered by the impartial hand of fate.

There is a solid basis for the "religion" of the Darwin Awards: Charles Darwin's theory of natural selection. In a single lifetime one finds ample proof that natural selection leads to evolution. We've seen evolution happen before our very eyes. Broccoli, dog breeds, nectarines, and modern corn all resulted from random mutations combined with natural (or artificial) selection.

Weeds provide an example of evolution happening in your own front lawn.

Dandelions are ubiquitous and very difficult to eliminate.

A handful of wild dandelion seeds will grow into adults of assorted heights, which scatter their seeds far and wide to begin the process again. But weekly lawn mowing schedules are a new selective pressure! We created a new environmental hazard for dandelions. And they rose, or rather shrunk, to meet the challenge.

Regular cutting of lawns selects for very short dandelions, ones that hug the ground too closely to be slashed by mower blades, and send up flowers that seed within days to avoid the reaper's scythe. A new short dandelion variant is branching off the general dandelion population. Over time the lawn dandelions may well diverge from the wild dandelions, increasingly specialized for the modern lawn environment, and a new species—the lawnlion?—will dawn.

Because examples of natural selection are easy to come by, the "religion" of the Darwin Awards stands on firm scientific footing. The interesting and powerful mechanism of natural selection is a blindly omniscient tool to increase the long-term survival of the human race—and provide a measure of immortality to comfort our transient personal existence.

> Robert Heinlein captured the poignancy of natural selection in his novel, *Time Enough for Love*: "Stupidity is the only universal capital crime; the sentence is death. There is no appeal, and execution is carried out automatically and without pity."

The stories that follow show the Darwinian repercussions to those who ignore religious strictures, and indulge in the seven deadly sins.

DARWIN AWARD: VANITY LIPOSUCTION TRAGEDY
Unconfirmed by Darwin
SEPTEMBER 1999, NEW YORK

David, a forty-four-year-old Mineola man, was more desperate to be rid of his flab than most. Why not save money and allow his friend to perform amateur liposuction on him in his garage? As you might guess, using a vacuum for liposuction is not the safest of weight loss programs. David died in the makeshift medical clinic, the victim of a lidocaine overdose. Anyone foolish enough to lie back and take the medical ministrations of a unlicensed liposuctionist in his garage workshop deserves to win a Darwin for heedless vanity.

The fake physician apologized to the man's family.

Reference: Associated Press

MORE VACUUM PERIL: Fantastic Plastic Lover, page 88

"I don't think, therefore I am not."

DARWIN AWARD: VANITY
PERILOUS POSE

Unconfirmed by Darwin

SEPTEMBER 2000, GERMANY

The picturesque medieval city of Rothenburg was recently the scene of a dramatic artistic effort. A fifty-three-year-old man from Baden-Würtemberg was posing nude in front of his camera, balanced atop a stone wall, when he lost his balance and fell sixteen feet to the ground below. Unlike its erstwhile owner, the camera remained safely settled on the tripod on the wall, and police plan to develop the film for clues to the man's death. Darwin anticipates that this story will stand as a testament to the self-pruning nature of the tree of life.

Reference: Ananova.com

ANOTHER POORLY FRAMED PHOTOGRAPH: Enraged Elephant, page 30

DARWIN AWARD: WRATH
THROWING STONES

Confirmed by Darwin

11 OCTOBER 2000, SAMARIA

The violent unrest in the Middle East has created a new Darwin Award winner. Three friends went to the Eli junction to enjoy a favorite activity: throwing stones at passing cars. They scored on a truck, then one walked into the street, stones in hand, to attack a passing car. The driver tried to swerve away from the man, lost control of his vehicle, and overturned, killing the stone thrower and severely injuring himself. Judea and Samaria district police jointly determined that the accidental crash was caused by the stone-throwing young men.

Those who live in glass houses shouldn't throw stones.

Reference: Ha'aretz, *ITIM*

THROWING SNOWBALLS: Snowball's Chance in Hell, page 73

An Iraqi terrorist didn't put enough postage on a letter bomb, and it came back marked "return to sender." He opened the package excitedly... and was rewarded with his own "surprise."
(Darwin Award nomination of unknown veracity, culled from a decade of email.)

DARWIN AWARD: GREED
CRYSTAL DAZE
2000, MEXICO *Confirmed by Darwin*

Chihuahua, Mexico, is home to two hot caverns containing the largest natural crystals known to man. "Walking into either of these caves is like stepping into a sweltering, gigantic geode," described one awed observer. Some of the clear crystals of selenite are over twenty feet long.

The newly discovered caverns buried twelve hundred feet below the surface of the earth carry a curse for those who seek to plunder their riches. A man recently tried to steal one of the magnificent crystals from the roof, and might have succeeded if he hadn't stood directly beneath it while chopping it free. He was crushed by the sparkling stalactite as it heeded the call of gravity.

Reference: Discovery Channel News

ANOTHER THIEF THWARTED BY A NATURAL FORCE:
Ferguson 2, Thieves 0, page 162

"To be or not to be . . ."

DARWIN AWARD: SLOTH
SLEEPFALLING

Confirmed by Darwin

19 JUNE 1999, AMSTERDAM

On a warm summer night in the Netherlands, an Italian resident who had picked up the habit of sleeping in the open air during sweltering Mediterranean summer nights decided to bed down on the roof. He climbed to the top of his apartment and arranged a comfortable bed, but paid little heed to the slope of the roof. Perhaps the night would have ended more happily if he had tucked himself in securely. Instead he fell asleep on top of his blanket, rolled down the incline, and plunged to his death.

Reference: *Mobile Alabama Press Register*

ANOTHER FATEFUL SNOOZE: Sheep Sleep, page 116

**A high IQ doesn't make up for
a lack of common sense.**

DARWIN AWARD: ENVY
FLAMES OF PASSION

Confirmed by Darwin

17 NOVEMBER 1999, GERMANY

Germany's image as a peaceful utopia has been tarnished by an acrimonious divorce. After bitter legal proceedings, Uwe of Brandenburg found that he had lost everything but his lederhosen knickerbockers. Among other possessions, the settlement demanded that Uwe turn over ownership of his house to his newly estranged wife.

Enraged by his wife's unmitigated legal victory, the forty-year-old man decided to follow the sage advice of an obscure German proverb: "If life gives you lemons, burn them."

Descending into the basement with his trusty drill, Uwe proceeded to bore several holes into a rather large oil tank. He then set fire to the fuel as it poured in erratic streams onto the floor. To his delight, the entire basement was engulfed in flames within seconds.

His joy turned to ashes, however, when he realized that he was now in the middle of a Hindenburg-sized house fire. Despite a valiant effort to save himself, Uwe died in the flames of his own vengeance. His wife got the last laugh.

Reference: *Düsseldorf Express*

MORE REVENGE GONE WRONG: Aircraft Airhead, page 35

DARWIN AWARD: ENVY
MOSCOW MARAUDER

Confirmed by Darwin

8 SEPTEMBER 2000, RUSSIA

A man who threatened to "deal with" his wife and her lover, instead dealt with himself in a revenge attempt gone wrong. He blew himself up with a homemade bomb in the far eastern Russian city of Khabarovsk. The device exploded when the man tried to attach it to the door of the lovers' not-so-secret apartment boudoir.

Reference: Reuters, Tass

🦎 MORE MEN PLAYING WITH BOMBS: Shell Shot, page 133

DARWIN AWARD: GLUTTONY
ETHANOL SCHMETHANOL

Unconfirmed by Darwin
MAY 2001, ENGLAND

> *We'll soon find out if I'm a scientist or not!*
> *I'll drop a pellet of the compound I created*
> *into this test tube...*

— Stan Lee's Spiderman, November 1963

With those murmured words, a Russian professor quaffed an aliquot of clear fluid from a beaker... and slowly succumbed to alcohol poisoning. The Oxford University professor had been in the habit of drinking laboratory ethanol, until he unwittingly poured his last drink from a bottle of methanol.

According to Usenet scientists, methanol is a common lab solvent that looks and smells like ethanol but is "five times as toxic and five times less intoxicating." Those who drink it invariably drink too much.

The forty-four-year-old professor of ecology was said to have had poor vision, and probably misread the label.

Reference: solstice.crest.org, *London Telegraph*

A GOPHER'S EXPERIENCE WITH MIND-ALTERING SUBSTANCES:
Revenge of the Gopher, page 203

The line between genius and stupidity is very fine.

HONORABLE MENTION: GLUTTONY
MEN EATING CHILI

Unconfirmed by Darwin

MAY 1999, PHILIPPINES

Three men attempting to land in the *Guinness Book of World Records* were hospitalized in Legaspi after eating excessive amounts of chili peppers. They were treated for acute gastritis and high blood pressure, and released with a warning to moderate their intake.

Reference: UPI, *The Star*

ANOTHER TRY FOR THE GUINNESS BOOK OF WORLD RECORDS: Rubbish, page 31
ANOTHER SERIOUS CASE OF INDIGESTION: The Last Supper, page 199

PERSONAL ACCOUNT: LUST
EMERGENCY ROOM EXCITEMENT

Back in 1984 I worked as a security guard in an Idaho hospital. One of my duties was to assist the emergency room staff with difficult patients. Late one Saturday night, I was paged to get to the emergency room STAT.

As I rushed down the corridor, I heard increasingly loud screams, but curiously, also laughter. I rounded the corner and nearly ran into a nurse leaning against the wall with a pan full of syringes. She was laughing so hard she was crying.

The ambulance had just brought in a very drunken individual, wearing nothing but a shirt and a bloody towel around his waist. He was too intoxicated and in too much pain to say what he had been doing, but his entire crotch area was filled with porcupine quills. It took the doctor the better part of three hours to remove them.

Reference: Don Cooley, personal account.

MORE EMERGENCY ROOM EXCITEMENT: Horsing Around, page 123; Tube Snake, page 107

Men with sexual proclivities for animals limit their contributions to the gene pool by turning their attentions to nonhuman partners—but men who are attracted to skunks are doubly "Darwinian" as they risk entirely losing their procreative abilities!

CHAPTER 2

Women:
Femme Fatalities

The moving finger writes, and having writ
moves on, nor all your piety nor wit
shall lure it back to cancel half a line.

—Omar Khayyam

Women make the world go round, but not the Darwin Awards. Rarely does the fair sex grace our annals! Here collected read every story of "Darwinian woman" in the book, fourteen in all. They comprise a group portrait of *Homo sapiens femme fatal*.

Discussion: Civilization Memes

The hand that rocks the cradle rules the world.

—William Ross Wallace

Genetic evolution is a fascinating concept, but a different kind of evolution is far more relevant to our daily lives: cultural evolution. Many critical discoveries that we exploit to shape our world have nothing to do with genetic changes. The domestication of animals, the smelting of copper, and the invention of writing have all dramatically altered our environment—and the methods we use to survive.

Humans learned to write less than six thousand years ago, as astoundingly recent as that sounds. Cognitive capacity developed for other survival purposes was adapted to a new use. The discovery that we could manipulate abstract ideas using concrete symbols, and in the process archive knowledge, revolutionized our lives. The change came from a cultural idea, and not a genetic elaboration.

Genetic changes proceed so slowly as to be imperceptible.* (See sidebar on page 28). Barring the emergence of a strong new selective pressure, it can take a hundred thousand years to mold a new species. But cultural evolution is rapid, and far more relevant to us on a day-to-day basis. It can alter our lives in the course of a millennium (as with agriculture), a generation (as with birth control), and, now that information propagates around the globe at the speed of the Internet, in a day.

We thrive in the vastly altered terrain of the modern world, adapting to new circumstances though our genes are substantially unchanged from ten thousand years ago—a time without modern technology. How is it possible for our culture to evolve so rapidly?

It is due to a unit of information called a *meme*. The meme, analogous to the genetic gene, is a self-propagating nugget of information with the capacity to infect and transform the thoughts of each person it encounters. It is our memes that allow current human circumstances to differ so dramatically from pre-technological civilization. This unseen agent of change is cloned, mutated, and spread through the medium of communication.

> *meme* (mēm) noun: A unit of information, such as a cultural practice or idea, transmitted from one mind to another in a self-propagating manner analogous to the replication of the genetic gene.

Language is a striking example of cultural evolution based on a highly contagious meme. Once held to be a spontaneous sudden mutation, it has been viewed more recently as resulting from "a simple case of humans tinkering around with the natural sounds of the mouth."** Perhaps humans, like infants, first communicated with a universally understood "babble" of simple concepts such as alarm and warmth, until the unbelievably powerful realization dawned that one could modulate sounds to express

---

**P. F. MacNeilage and B. L. Davis, "Motor explanations of babbling and early speech patterns," *Developmental Neurocognition: Speech and face processing in first year of life* by Boysson-Bardies B. et al (1993).

complex concepts. The notion of language was so useful that it spread quickly from group to group, each inventing their own words and perhaps creating, as a side effect, the confusion of the Tower of Babel.

Memes can also be spread nonverbally. A tossed ball conveys the idea that objects can be transmitted without continuous hand to hand contact. Cave paintings, pantomime, and teaching by doing are all ways of transferring memes without language. But language is a particularly adept agent of meme infection because it can more easily convey complex abstractions to a wider audience.

Our brains are able to produce and exploit language and writing because we are capable of abstract thought. Next time you make a statement about your views, think about the memes it contains—and which are of your own invention. We each generate and replicate memes as readily as we breathe air.

*Is evolution slow? Punctuated Equilibrium Theory says no!
www.DarwinAwards.com/book/equilibrium.html
The chronology of technology.:
www.DarwinAwards.com/book/technochrono.html

Our civilization flourishes on the topological mindscape of our memes. Thus it is no coincidence that women, long recognized for their role in passing our culture from generation to generation, excel at spreading memes. The stories that follow feature women who can no longer pass along certain unprofitable memes—particularly those relating to poor risk assessment!

DARWIN AWARD: FAST FOOD FATALITY

Confirmed by Darwin

3 SEPTEMBER 2000, INDIANA

The felonious antics of two fast-food franchise managers ended tragically when their robbery cover-up scheme went up in smoke. Lisa, twenty-two-year-old night manager of a Burger King, conspired with a coworker to heist over $4,000 from the restaurant.

They staged an elaborate fake robbery/arson, in which Lisa acted the part of the victim bound with duct tape and trapped in the walk-in meat cooler, while her co-conspirator started a small fire and walked off with a duffel bag of cash. A key part of their plan was a quick "rescue" of Lisa by the local fire department.

Unfortunately the wastebasket fire went unnoticed until the morning shift arrived to find a slow-burning smolder that had never erupted into the desired blaze. The air from the open door caused the smolder to burst into flames, and firefighters were summoned. They found Lisa in the freezer, chilled and semi-conscious, and rushed her to a hospital where she died from hypothermia.

Lisa's body showed no signs of forced restraint, the duct tape was loose, and she could have easily freed herself from her bindings and escaped from the unlocked refrigerator.

Reference: thetimesonline.com

ANOTHER HYPOTHERMIC DEATH: Fishing with No Compass, page 46

DARWIN AWARD: ENRAGED ELEPHANT
Unconfirmed by Darwin
7 JANUARY 2001, TANZANIA

Yet another safari tourist met with an early demise when she left the safety of the tour bus, in the face of numerous explicit warnings, in order to frame a better picture. The woman, a volunteer with the Peace Corps, and her camera were fatally trampled by an enraged elephant in Ruaha National Park. Let her fate remind you to "keep your arms and legs inside the vehicle at all times."

Reference: South African Press Association

ANOTHER FATEFUL PHOTO OPPORTUNITY: Perilous Pose, page 15

**"I find it the greatest pity
that she had thought to use contraceptives
before her mother. . . ."**

DARWIN AWARD: RUBBISH!

Confirmed by Darwin

1 MARCH 2000, NEW ZEALAND

Baldwin Street in Dunedin is listed as the steepest in the world in the *Guinness Book of World Records*, and it was at the top of this thirty-eight-degree incline that two women hatched a plan for a midnight downhill slide.

The two university students dragged a two-wheeled rubbish bin up the street, climbed in, shoved off, and down they went in their makeshift sleigh. As they hurtled pell-mell down Baldwin Street in the wee hours of the morning, residents described being awakened by "a hell of a racket" which went on for some time before ending with a sickening crash.

Their fifty-meter dash ended precipitously when the rubbish bin slammed into a legally parked trailer. One student, nineteen, was killed instantly, and her copilot suffered serious head injuries—though one wonders how they noticed.

The feat did not make it into the *Guinness Book of World Records*, as the top speed of the rubbish bin is unknown.

References: *New Zealand Herald*, Reuters
ANOTHER FATAL CRASH: Metallica Concert Misadventure, page 205

DARWIN AWARD: CHRISTMAS TREE

Unconfirmed by Darwin

25 NOVEMBER 2000, CANADA

A sixty-six-year-old Quebec woman was hit not once, not twice, but three times by speeding cars on a Canadian highway while trying to save her Christmas trees. Yes, trees. The woman had been driving on the highway with several conifers strapped none-too-securely to the roof of her car, when they slipped from their moorings and fell onto the traffic lanes.

It was nighttime and there were no lights on the road, but nevertheless the courageous woman risked, and lost, her life in a vain attempt to rescue her trees from the speeding cars.

Reference: *Le Nouvelliste*, Trois-Rivières, Canada

ANOTHER TRAFFIC IMPACT: Scooter Snuff, page 69

Philosophical question: would she still be eligible for a Darwin if she was doing a public service by removing the obstacles from the road?

DARWIN AWARD: TESTING FAITH

Confirmed by Darwin

27 OCTOBER 2000, ILLINOIS

A splinter religious group that tests their faith by standing in traffic lost one of their members when she was struck by a vehicle on Interstate 55 while professing her beliefs to the passing motorists. It was not her first attempt to win converts in the middle of the busy freeway, but it was certainly her last.

Reference: "News of the Weird," *Springfield State Journal-Register*

MORE RELIGIOUS FAITHFUL: Walking on Water, page 49

Theology-minded readers submitted these
illuminating biblical quotes:

"You must not put Jehovah to the test."
—Matthew 4:7

"Neither let us put Jehovah to the test."
—1 Corinthians 10:9

DARWIN AWARD: THAT SINKING FEELING
Confirmed by Darwin
16 FEBRUARY 2001, FLORIDA

Karla, thirty-two, fell asleep at the wheel and drove her car into a thirty-foot-deep canal. Alarmed by her predicament, she dialed 911 from her cell phone. The operator urged her to roll down her windows or open the door, but she refused. "If I do, all the water is going to come in!"

If you are unlucky enough to find yourself trapped in a sinking car, it is essential to roll the windows down immediately so that you can escape from the vehicle. Once the bottom of your door is even slightly submerged, the water pressure makes it almost impossible to open the door until the car is nearly full, which equalizes the pressure.

It takes a car up to ten minutes to sink, depending on how well sealed the vehicle is, but the electrical system may fail much sooner if the water penetrates the body and short-circuits the wires. In most cars with automatic windows, the motor that powers the window is located halfway up the car door, so you must act fast if you plan to survive.

Karla was a strong swimmer and could have paddled to safety, if only she had managed to escape from her vehicle. When Karla and her 1998 BMW were pulled from the canal, they found the keys to the ignition in her purse, and the left rear window entirely open.

Reference: *Miami Herald*

MORE INFORMATION ABOUT THE DANGERS OF CARS: Car Safety, page 58

HONORABLE MENTION: AIRCRAFT AIRHEAD

Unconfirmed by Darwin

29 JANUARY 2001, GUYANA

There's a time and a place for everything. But attacking your ex-lover with a knife while he is piloting a plane in midair is generally regarded as both the wrong time and the wrong place. Particularly by the other occupants of the aircraft.

Karol Ann, twenty-one, was "suffering from a broken heart" when she stabbed her ex-lover and current pilot in the neck and shoulder. Fortunately for all concerned, a female passenger flying with her nine-year-old daughter wrested the knife from Jennifer's hand, and the wounded pilot managed to land the four-seat Cessna plane safely.

Could she possibly have been unaware of the danger of attacking an aircraft pilot while in midair? Whether ignorant or suicidal, Karol Ann, who makes her living as "a star reporter," is advised to stick to writing headlines instead of making them.

More misguided revenge: Flames of Passion, page 19

**Genius may have its limitations,
but stupidity is not thus handicapped.**

DARWIN AWARD: FATAL FOOTWEAR FASHION
Confirmed by Darwin
2 NOVEMBER 1999, TOKYO

Platform shoes, that must-have fashion accessory for young women, have already claimed two lives. More deaths are predicted if women continue to totter in their footsteps.

The first victim was a twenty-five-year-old nursery school teacher who died in her car after suffering a skull fracture from a fall from thirteen-centimeter platform sandals. The second victim crashed her vehicle into a concrete pole, unable to hit the brake pedal because her eight-centimeter heels got in the way. Sadly her innocent passenger died.

In light of recent tragedies, experts are urging the public to take steps to prevent such dire platform mishaps, as well as less fatal but still painful foot and back injuries. With the soles of some shoes reaching as high as thirty centimeters, health police are asking concerned citizens to warn fashion-minded friends and family to "just say no" before a platform shoe mishap befalls them.

Reference: *San Francisco Guardian, National Post*

ANOTHER EXAMPLE OF APPEARANCE TAKING PRECEDENCE OVER BRAINS:
Show-Off, page 52

HONORABLE MENTION: EXPLOSIVE MIX OF GIRLS
Confirmed by Darwin
14 MARCH 2000, DENMARK

Three teenage girls were hanging out in the public rest room sniffing lighter fluid gas, when one of them casually lit a cigarette. The explosion ignited the fumes filling the small enclosure, and the girls rushed from the toilets—straight into the arms of police, because the rest room they had chosen was in the same building as the police station.

Inspector Leif Høy said, "We heard a bang from the toilets. A moment later the girls ran out screaming." The officers gave them first aid by dousing them with cold water, and sent them to the hospital for further treatment.

None of the gas-sniffing girls was in danger of losing her life, but unless they learn a few permanent lessons from this experience, we expect to hear from them again.

- Lesson One: When sniffing lighter fluid, avoid doing so next to a police station, unless you foresee the need for first aid.
- Lesson Two: When sniffing lighter fluid in a small closed room, try to control the urge for nicotine until you are well away from the fumes.
- Lesson Three: Do not sniff lighter fluid.

Reference: *Politiken*, Denmark

ANOTHER STORY IN THE VICINITY OF A TOILET: Toilet Trap, page 102

HONORABLE MENTION: SNOW BUNNIES
Confirmed by Darwin
JANUARY 2001, ONTARIO, CANADA

In the middle of winter snow season, Susan, nineteen, and Wendy, twenty-one, got lost driving along snowy highways in a rural part of Canada. One wrong turn led to another, and the girls eventually found themselves wandering aimlessly along "seasonal trails" marked KEEP OUT and NO TRESPASSING.

After becoming hopelessly lost, they inadvertently set fire to their car while trying to dislodge it from a rock. The girls abandoned the vehicle and its survival kit, containing a blanket, flashlight, candle, and flares. The two snow bunnies struck out on their own and stumbled blindly through the trees for two hours, until they broke through an ice cover and fell into a stream. They were discovered trapped there by a rabbit hunter twelve hours later.

Between them, the women lost two feet, seven additional toes, and four fingers to frostbite.

Reference: Halifax *Chronicle-Herald*
🐾 ANOTHER SNOW STORY: Two Avalanche Alaskan, page 63

HONORABLE MENTION: DUMB DRUNK

Unconfirmed by Darwin

FEBRUARY 2001, CONNECTICUT

A woman arrested on a drunken driving charge made an odd choice when calling for a ride home. Betty used her one phone call to contact Ken, her drinking companion prior to her arrest, who was visibly drunk when he staggered into police headquarters.

Ken failed a sobriety test. More surprisingly, a routine background check revealed that Betty had recently obtained a legal restraining order against him. A police sergeant explained, "We cannot allow him to come into contact with her—even if she says it's okay."

Ken was charged with violating a restraining order and driving while intoxicated. One question remains—was Betty or Ken the more foolish of the pair?

Reference: *Hartford Courant*

MORE DRUNKEN BEHAVIOR: Sobriety Test, page 168

**Evolution: Taking care of those
too stupid to take care of themselves.**

PERSONAL ACCOUNT: EAT THE YOUNG
OCTOBER 2000, WYOMING

One day a ranger for the Yellowstone National Park Service joined a crowd of people, cars, trucks, and motor homes that had congregated to watch a bear. One woman and her little boy stood out in the crowd. She was smearing something unidentifiable all over the boy's face.

The ranger asked the woman what she was doing.

She answered, "Putting honey on him, of course!"

Stunned, he asked the obvious question: Why?

She answered matter-of-factly, "I want to take a picture of the bear licking it off his face!"

Fortunately for the child, but perhaps unfortunately from an evolutionary standpoint, the ranger prevented the child from approaching the bear. To this day he has nightmares about it. This event just goes to show why some animals feel compelled to eat their own young in the wild.

Reference: Gene Leone, personal account.

A DIFFERENT KIND OF RUN-IN WITH AUTHORITIES: Miracle Mile, page 81

PERSONAL ACCOUNT: BRUSH WITH STUPIDITY
DECEMBER 2000

Necessity is the mother of invention. Necessity is also the mother of severe injury. My husband was on his way to work when he pulled to a stop at a traffic light. He noticed that the occupant of the car behind him was holding a lighter up in the air and flicking it on and off, on and off. His curiosity got the better of him, and he maneuvered closer to her at the next light to see what she was doing.

The woman was holding sections of her hair over the lighter's flame in a ridiculous attempt to dry it. I am certain this individual will be gracing the pages of the Darwin Awards soon. Ingenuity of that caliber is sure to rear its head again.

Reference: Sarah and Paul Melancon, personal account.

A MORE DANGEROUS FLAME: Scuba Divers and Forest Fires, page 208

More Femme Fatalities
www.DarwinAwards.com/book/femme.html

CHAPTER 3

Water:
All Washed Up

*Better to remain silent and be thought a fool
than to speak out and remove all doubt.*

—Abraham Lincoln

Our bodies are more liquid than solid, yet we have
forgotten a surprising amount about water in our
climb out of the primeval ooze. Here's why you
should avoid submerging your head for prolonged
periods.

DISCUSSION: WEED SEEDS AND BIODIVERSITY

Think about weed seeds. They come in a plethora of varieties, tall and short, early and late blooming, quick and slow to germinate. A handful of local weed seeds is guaranteed to have a few that are suitable for growth in any given patch of fertile ground.

This is quite unlike the uniform characteristics of our inbred crop and flower strains. From a packet of a thousand garden marigold seeds, all but a few plants will be identical in size and flower structure. That would never happen with a handful of weed seeds. Even weedy, undomesticated marigolds grow in a wide diversity of forms. They are tall, short, and stunted; one grows more foliage while another sets more blossoms.

Our domesticated seeds are selected to yield plants that germinate, flower, and senesce in tandem. How did that come to be? A breeder takes a wild stock and selects the offspring that best suit his criteria. Eventually the genetic variation of the plant is reduced, and a true-breeding variety is established.

Recent forays into cloning—inserting desirable genes into crops—are a logical extension of traditional breeding methods. The curiosity and desire to improve food crops that drove hundreds of generations of effort is still operating today, now that we have the means to insert foreign genes of benefit into our crop species.

The trouble with inbred crop lines, whether produced by cloning or by traditional methods, is that they are less robust. Throw a handful of crop corn seeds onto a terrain with varied habitats. The seeds will not fare as well as an equal number taken from wild corn strains with more diversity. They are overspecialized.

Overspecialization caused by reduced genetic diversity illustrates one of the dangers of allowing wild species to die out. There are wild food plants with more protein, more insect resistance, and different flavors than we have in our fields today. There are wild cattle with more resistance to disease and to drought. We need to be able to reach into a deep gene pool from time to time, in order to reinvigorate our specialized domestic varieties.

So the next time you see a weed seed, appreciate it for its unique and random character. Biodiversity is a treasure beyond compare.

Genetically Engineered Crops: Pro and Con
www.DarwinAwards.com/book/cropclone.html

A diverse gene pool serves as a valuable repository of useful and successful genetic traits. Biodiversity is far less appealing, however, when it is salted with undesirable traits. The Darwin nominees in this chapter are, in their own small way, reducing the biodiversity of our species—but in a manner for which we are all eternally grateful.

DARWIN AWARD: FISHING WITH NO COMPASS

Unconfirmed by Darwin

MARCH 2001, OHIO

Lake Erie claimed three more victims who were hoping to catch a few fish but instead caught a fatal chill. "Someone noticed tracks leading to a [fishing] hole and an ice chest floating in the water," said Deputy Sheriff Roger Garn.

The three men had been driving on a thin sheet of ice surrounded by open patches of water, which they may have overlooked due to poor visibility caused by a morning snowstorm. Suddenly, to no one's surprise but theirs, their all-terrain vehicle plunged through the weak ice. Hours later divers rescued the bodies from ten feet of thirty-four-degree water.

The winters had not been cold enough to allow ice fishing on the lake for three years, and authorities had warned the public about the unsafe conditions. In January, twenty anglers had been rescued from a patch of ice that broke away from shore. Yet even the recent deaths did little to deter fishermen.

Deputy Sheriff Garn said bemusedly, "We're taking three people off in body bags, and [dozens] were still going [past us] to fish."

Reference: Associated Press

🎣 ANOTHER STORY ABOUT FISHING: FISH GAG, PAGE 115

DARWIN AWARD: DUCT TAPE

Confirmed by Darwin

24 APRIL 2000, OREGON

A misplaced faith in the miracle of duct tape led to the demise of a man boating on the Columbia River.

Duct tape has a reputation for fixing any problem. Steven and a friend were fishing in a twelve-foot aluminum boat held together with multiple duct tape repairs, including the motor mount. Suddenly they encountered rough water and Steven stood up in the boat.

The overtaxed duct tape gave way, and the vessel, rated to hold 200 pounds, capsized and tossed the two men and their 640 pounds of equipment into the water.

The U.S. Coast Guard rescued the surviving companion the next morning, but Steven was not so lucky. He was found dead in an ill-fitting life jacket. Perhaps if he had duct taped it in place, he would still be sailing the river in his rickety dinghy, instead of holding a Darwin Award.

Reference: KOIN 6 News

ANOTHER USE FOR DUCT TAPE: Fast Food Fatality, page 29

Another Sap from the Tree of Life

DARWIN AWARD: DODGING DRINK DUES

Unconfirmed by Darwin

15 MAY 2001, EGYPT

Two whiskey-swilling men tried to dodge their bar tab by down-ing one last drink, jumping in the Nile, and swimming for the far shore. One, a twenty-seven-year-old taxi driver, misjudged his ability to stay afloat. He drowned en route, successfully avoiding paying the $180 bill. His companion reached the far shore a few hundred meters away, only to be arrested by Cairo police who had been summoned by the shortchanged nightclub employees.

Next time you and your friends try to dodge a bar tab, don't drink yourself senseless first. You might die or, even more dread-ful, be stuck with the entire bar tab!

Reference: Agence France Presse

🐾 MORE SENSELESS DROWNINGS: Count Your Chickens, page 198

A twenty-seven-year-old policeman fell to his death when he accidentally piloted a powerful speedboat over 165-foot high Loskop Dam near Johannesburg.

(Darwin Award nomination of unknown veracity,
culled from a decade of email.)

DARWIN AWARD: WALKING ON WATER

Confirmed by Darwin

24 NOVEMBER 1999, CALIFORNIA

One sect of Christians attempted to follow in Jesus' footsteps more literally than most. They worked to master the secret of walking on water. Diligently, day after day, the group tried to be closer to God by making a sincere effort to walk on water. These Christians continued their unorthodox practices until the leader of the small group unexpectedly died while practicing in his bathtub. His wife said James spent many hours trying to perfect the technique of walking on water, but had not yet mastered the ability. He apparently drowned after slipping on a bar of soap, proving that walking on water does bring one closer to God.

References: EAP, cyberramp.net

ANOTHER ACT OF GOD: God Saves? page 91

> Anyone can walk on water. I've done it myself.
> Just wait until the lake freezes. . .

DARWIN AWARD: DIVE TO DEATH

Confirmed by Darwin

4 JULY 1998, TEXAS

If you fly over Houston, you will see the sky-blue rectangles of countless backyard swimming pools. A Houston man joined the club and purchased his own aboveground pool on June 21, 1998. He selected the location, and the pool was installed by an independent contractor a few days later. He rated all aspects of the installation as "excellent."

A few weeks later, the pool owner was swimming with his friends and enjoying an alcoholic Fourth of July haze in the humid Houston heat. In an unprecedented show of bravado, the man decided to climb onto the patio roof and dive into his new pool.

The man was six feet tall. His pool, typical for an aboveground model, was four feet deep. So when his head hit the bottom, his legs were still sticking two feet out of the water. The dive broke his neck.

He sued on the grounds of faulty installation and inappropriate location. Yes, the same installation the man had rated as "excellent," placed in the location he himself had selected.

The pool owner passed away in December. Next time you fly over Houston and see those miles of swimming pools, remember the story of this man's last, miscalculated dive.

Reference: A source at the pool installation company

DEATH FROM A DIFFERENT LIQUID: Ethanol Schmethanol, page 21

DARWIN AWARD: PASSIONATE PLUNGE
Confirmed by Darwin
JULY 1998, ENGLAND

A man with the unlikely ambition to jump off every river bridge in Norwich ended his athletic career with a seventy-foot leap into three feet of water. Friends said the thirty-four-year-old man had fulfilled his dream of jumping off every city bridge spanning the River Wensum. Having exhausted the bridge selection, this time he climbed to the top of a multi-story car park, looked down from the parapets, and shouted an inquiry to onlookers asking how deep the water was. Then he plunged to his death in the shallow waters below. Emergency workers were unable to resuscitate the man, who was said to possess "a strange and unusual passion for jumping into rivers."

Reference: MSN News, UK Electronic Telegraph
ANOTHER DISASTROUS FALL: The Bricklayer, page 103

**If at first you don't succeed . . .
then skydiving is not for you.**

DARWIN AWARD: SHOW-OFF

Unconfirmed by Darwin

AUGUST 1999, ENGLAND

A twenty-seven-year-old man bent on impressing three boys dove into the ocean from an eighty-foot cliff. He was knocked unconscious by the impact with the water. One of the boys, unimpressed, climbed down the cliff and dragged the man from the sea while his friends called for help.

The impetuous man was airlifted from Skrinkle Haven to Withybush Hospital in Haverfordwest, where he was declared dead on arrival. Police reported that that the rescuer, an eleven-year-old boy, acted very bravely. His fourteen-year-old comrades were also commended for their presence of mind, made all the more notable by the absence of mind displayed by the adult.

Reference: Yahoo!

EQUALLY COURAGEOUS BUT LESS SENSIBLE BOYS:
Polar Bear Lesson, page 121

Slovenia's state-run news agency reported the death of a fisherman, forty-seven, who drowned after hooking a huge lake sheatfish and refusing to let go as he waded in and was pulled under. Friends reported his last words were "Now I've got him!" Divers found his body after a two-day search.

. (Darwin Award nomination of unknown veracity,
culled from a decade of email.)

HONORABLE MENTION: ALL ABOARD

Unconfirmed by Darwin

17 SEPTEMBER 2000, AUSTRALIA

Six young men and women with no sailing experience were rescued from a stolen luxury yacht after drifting into a pier only four hundred meters from the boat's mooring.

They had intended to sail around the world, and had packed all the essentials: sixty cans of baked beans, one thousand condoms, some liquor and cola, and a library book on navigating by the stars. Luckily for them they were caught, as police report that "they had no fresh water and no food other than baked beans."

The would-be sailors have been charged with unlawful use of a vessel. We can all be glad that at least with a thousand condoms, they weren't planning to breed.

Reference: *Victoria Sunday Herald*

ANOTHER STORY OF PLANS THWARTED BY INEXPERIENCE: Do It Yourself, Do Yourself In, page 61

HONORABLE MENTION: SEWER SHOWER

Unconfirmed by Darwin

JANUARY 2001, ENGLAND

Flooding problems at Tangmere gave an opportunistic young vandal a good idea, or so it seemed at the time. Expecting to create a spectacular fountain of water, he disconnected a drainage pipe—only to have his pride drenched with liquefied human waste, as the drainage pipe he had selected was connected to an overflowing septic tank. Although he lived to tell the tale, his malodorous shower indicates that this young man may well find a Darwin Award in his future.

ANOTHER MISCREANT REDOLENT WITH MUCK: **Toilet Trap, page 102**

Celibacy is not hereditary.
Stupidity is.

URBAN LEGEND: BREWERY MISHAP
MAY 2000, AUSTRALIA

My great-uncle worked at a brewery in Melbourne around the turn of the century. Whilst inspecting one of the tanks, he lost his footing and fell headlong into the vat.

This is more dangerous than it sounds. Beer contains ethanol, which has a lower density than water. He was unable to swim to the surface, and drowned before rescuers could assist him.

The worst thing about it, they say, is that the entire batch of beer had to be thrown out with him. Quite true.

ANOTHER CAUTIONARY LEGEND: Frog Giggin' Accident, page 204

Is it possible to drown in beer? Of course it's *possible* to drown in a saucer of water, therefore it's technically possible to drown in a vat of beer. But do the physical properties of beer make it more likely?

Ethanol has a specific gravity less than water, which means you would not float as readily, if at all. But some say that beer, which is only a few percent alcohol, has a specific gravity greater than water. During the fermentation, specific gravity changes as sugar is converted to alcohol, but solutes such as carbohydrates are always present to increase the liquid's density. In that case you would be more buoyant in beer.

Then again, carbon dioxide bubbles might *lower* its specific gravity.

Certain brews might be so viscous that it would be as tiring as swimming in quicksand.

And would a reduced surface tension have any effect?

Do breweries really contain open vats of beer?

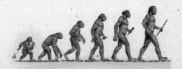

It has been suggested that carbon dioxide given off by the yeast in the fermenting liquor might settle on top of the vat, suffocating a hapless swimmer. The gas might even be retained in the beer tank's thick layer of foam. CO_2 is heavier than air and has been observed to accumulate in the still air of ancient caves and in lakes whose "burps" kill entire towns.

You can perform a CO_2 experiment yourself. Collect the fumes from a burning match in a small bowl held below the flame. Then "dunk" the match in the invisible gas, or pour it over a lit candle, to extinguish the flame.

Whether or not you believe this story is possible, there are worse ways to die than drowning in a huge vat of booze.

Mull over the science behind the Brewery Mishap.
www.DarwinAwards.com/book/brewery.html

Gravity: More than a good idea—it's the law!

CHAPTER 4

Technology:
Engines of Destruction

The total IQ of the world is a constant.
The more people, the more idiots.

We evolved from living in trees to living amongst modern machinery ... but some men haven't yet made that evolutionary leap. Here's a primer on the dangers of our own devices.

DISCUSSION: CAR SAFETY

Consider the dangers you face from cars. One of the best ways to assure your continued health is to avoid automobiles. Each time you drive or walk along the street, you trust your life to strangers in metal juggernauts. Car wrecks injure and kill far more frequently than lightning, yet the distant rumble of thunder causes more terror than the nearby rumble of a car engine. Exhaust fumes cause health and environmental problems. The interiors of cars, particularly when new, exude unpleasant volatile chemicals. Cars are the source of many hazards.

The significant dangers posed by automobiles can be minimized by eliminating them from our environment altogether. Although that seems unlikely to happen in the next twenty years, less drastic measures can be taken now to reduce your risks from motor vehicles.

When you buy a car, look for airbags front and sides, antilock brakes, seat belts, childproof locks, and reinforced frames. These features make the modern car safer than ever. Even if you have little money, it is worth your health to buy a car with as many safety features as possible. Cell phones for emergency calls also can be an important part of automotive safety.

Safety improvements don't come without some risks. Airbags can break bones and noses. Cell phone distractions maim and kill many drivers. But the overall incidence of injury and death is greatly reduced by safety innovations. They provide such significant improvements that it's madness to spend much time in a car without them.

New safety features help reduce physical trauma, but don't address the environmental concerns posed by manufacturing processes and vehicle emissions.

Cars emit chemical plasticizers from synthetic surfaces inside the vehicle. Over time the release of fumes abates, but when the car is new, volatile gases are fairly concentrated. To minimize exposure, keep the windows rolled down and occasionally wipe hard surfaces with a mild cleaning solution to remove chemical films.

Cars pour out greenhouse gases that contribute to global warming. Every gallon of gas you burn dumps twenty pounds of CO_2 into the atmosphere. Incomplete combustion produces carbon monoxide, toxic hydrocarbons, and nitrogen oxides. They in turn produce acid rain and ground-level ozone, our most intractable urban air pollution problem.

As a society we are not taking sufficient heed of the garbage accumulating in our atmosphere, much of it spewed from our cars. We are polluting the earth faster than it can recover.

Perhaps we shouldn't worry. This is not the first monumental change the atmosphere has undergone. When the earth was younger, photosynthetic plants began to fill the air with oxygen. Oxygen is a highly reactive molecule, and for a billion years it was sequestered in the form of iron oxides, or rust. But eventually the amount of oxygen produced by plants exceeded the earth's ability to sequester it.

As oxygen built up in the atmosphere, it forever altered the kinds of lifeforms that could exist in the open air. We are one of those lifeforms. But the majority of species then alive were fatally poisoned and have never been seen again.

Perhaps we will one day create an atmosphere in which we can no longer survive, and other species will evolve to make use of (or be protected from) the outgassing of our civilization.

If we're lucky we might evolve fast enough to survive in our own effluvium. But don't, or rather do, hold your breath! The stories that follow show that we have a ways to go before we can even cope with saws, forklifts, and electricity.

Darwin Awards: Too Stupid to Live

DARWIN AWARD:
DO IT YOURSELF, DO YOURSELF IN

Confirmed by Darwin

2000, COLORADO

Summer is the most blissful of seasons, when our favorite summertime activity—do it yourself stupidity—kicks into high gear. Meet Charles, thirty-four, a Denver masonry contractor who created brick and mortar edifices.

Charles was in construction. He had worked on houses, and he had watched electricians install wiring. He believed this qualified him as a member of the Junior Electrician Society. He figured he could handle any electrical issue that came up around his own home.

One day on the job Charles was apparently bonked in the head by his bricks. He had a great idea! He would build an electric fence in his own backyard. An electric fence to keep the dogs in, and keep the puppy paternity cases down.

Charles connected a wire to an extension cord and circled his backyard with a 120-volt strand of electrified copper without mishap. The household became accustomed to the jury-rigged security system, and things settled down to normal, until Charles picked up a passion for gardening.

Charles had a sizable crop of backyard produce. On harvest day he reached for a tomato, put his hand on the electrified wire, and . . . there's really no need to explain what happened next.

Why did Charles expire? Like other inexperienced amateurs, he thought he knew what he was doing, but his design had two

major flaws. Electrified dog fences use one-tenth the voltage of cattle fences, and he needed to install a repeater that transmitted 150-microsecond pulses. That's how you can safely hit a cow with a jolt of juice—it cuts off in time to avoid creating a pile of rare steaks by the fence.

The moral of this story is, as always, one of the guiding principles of common sense: if you don't know how to do something, don't do it!

Reference: *Greater Denver Rocky Mountain News*

ANOTHER AMATEUR ELECTRICIAN: **Power Punch Proves Fatal, page 68**

An ISCET-certified electrician on safety: "An electric fence is not 'one-tenth of 120 volts'—if it were, you could shock yourself touching the terminals of a car battery. An electric fence is normally a few thousand volts. Low amperage is why animals and people aren't killed when they touch it. It's similar to getting a static shock from a TV screen: the voltage could be as high as 50,000 volts (five times higher than an electric fence's standard charge) and still be safe. UL and CSA certify that without continuous amperage, there can be no damage. Anyone who cares to make an electric fence had better make note of this information."

Does he have his facts straight?
www.DarwinAwards.com/book/electricity.html

DARWIN AWARD: TWO AVALANCHE ALASKAN

Confirmed by Darwin

8 APRIL 2000, ALASKA

Ordinarily a man killed by an avalanche is suffering from bad luck, and not eligible for a Darwin Award. But the circumstances surrounding the death of Walter, a forty-three-year-old Fairbanks man, are unusual enough to warrant an exception. He was killed not by a natural disaster, but by his own blatant stupidity.

Walter was in the Summit Lake area for the annual Arctic Man Ski & Sno Go Classic, which combines skis and snow machines with pristine ice. To celebrate the event, he was highmarking the mountains with his snow machine. This stunt involves driving as far as possible up the side of a mountain and, just before the machine bogs down from the ascent, turning and driving back down. The U-shaped furrow on the hill marks your best shot until a buddy takes a charge up the hill and betters it. Highmarkers like to do it above tree level so everybody can see their display of testosterone.

Using heavy and noisy machines to undermine the snowpack in an avalanche-prone area is not a sport for the meek. The warm spring weather had destabilized the snow and caused several avalanches, and event organizers urged recreational snowmachiners to stay off the steep slopes. Walter himself had been buried waist-deep in an avalanche that day, and had been warned by rescuing State Troopers to stay off the mountains, or at least carry an avalanche beacon.

But their warnings and Walter's own substantial experience with snow machines were not enough to save him. The avalanche that ended his life was an unstable slab of wind-deposited snow resting on a layer of temperature-weakened snow. Avalanche expert Jill Fredston pinpointed likely search locations, and rescue dogs Chili and Bean located the frozen victim lying faceup under four feet of snow.

Sergeant Paul Burke said, "You'd think people would have more prudence." Some people do, but not a Darwin Award winner like Walter.

Reference: *Anchorage Daily News*
TWO SNOW-COVERED WOMEN: Snow Bunnies, page 38

Stupidity is a sexually transmitted disease.

DARWIN AWARD: FORKLIFT SAFETY VIDEO

2000 Darwin Award Winner
Confirmed by Darwin
11 MARCH 2000, AUSTRALIA

It just stands to reason that one should follow safe practices while filming a safety video, but Peter, the fifty-two-year-old owner of a machinery and equipment training school in Perth, violated that rule of common sense while filming a forklift safety demonstration.

With the cameras rolling, he piloted the forklift across the yard, lost traction on a patch of loose gravel, and was thrown from the cabin and crushed. Subsequent investigation confirmed that the factors responsible for the fatality were driver error in using high speed over varied terrain, coupled with the imprudent decision to omit a seat belt.

Peter's final safety demonstration was the most convincing of his career.

Reference: ABC News Online, safetynews.com

ANOTHER VIDEO TAKES A NASTY TURN: Rappin' on Heaven's Door, page 87

Three Malaysian executioners manning the gallows accidentally hanged themselves while clowning around. The most recent mishap occurred when an executioner preparing for an upcoming sentence slipped the noose around his neck. He was having his picture taken when the gallows' trapdoor gave way, breaking his neck.

(Darwin Award nomination of unknown veracity, culled from a decade of email.)

DARWIN AWARD: ELECTRIFYING STUNT
Unconfirmed by Darwin
1995, MICHIGAN

Up here in Michigan, seems some poor fellow thought it would be a good idea to "move" a downed wire from his car. Newspaper reports say it took a *full minute* of neighbors whacking away at him with a two-by-four to free their freshly fried former friend from the fatal flashing.

A STORY ABOUT LESS CONGENIAL NEIGHBORS: A Medieval Tale, page 139

Darwin Awards: Gene Pool Belly Flops

DARWIN AWARD: INTERSECTING DARWINS

Confirmed by Darwin

15 APRIL 2001, TENNESSEE

The day before the U.S. tax filing deadline, a Memphis Darwin Award winner trying to beat a train drove around the crossing gates—only to be struck by an oncoming vehicle whose driver had the same mad plan. The occupants of one vehicle were killed, making this monumental stupidity the first instance we have witnessed of a Darwin Award winner crashing into an Honorable Mention. The accident happened to one side of the tracks, so the train passed by unimpeded.

Reference: *Memphis Commercial Appeal*

MORE TRAIN HUMOR: Chicken with a Train, page 101

DARWIN AWARD: POWER PUNCH PROVES FATAL

Unconfirmed by Darwin

AUGUST 1999, ENGLAND

Ian was a fitness fanatic and self-employed electrician living in an English seaside town. He had recently converted one room of his cottage into a new gym. Among the weights and exercise equipment hung a punching bag, suspended by a chain from the ceiling.

Little did Ian realize that he had inadvertently managed to combine his hobby with his work. After a Saturday night carousing with his cousin, Ian came home to show off his new gym. Leading the way, he switched on the lights and casually punched the punching bag. He was knocked to the floor by a bolt of electricity and died instantly.

He had wired the power supply to the punching bag.

Ian's best friend said: "He was a brilliant guy. It's crazy that two major parts of his life contributed to his death." You might say he was shockingly fit.

Reference: *London Evening Standard, Weston Daily Press*

ANOTHER FELLOW SHOWING OFF TO FRIENDS: Passionate Plunge, page 51

Darwin Awards: Population Control Volunteers

Darwin Award: Scooter Snuff

Confirmed by Darwin

25 January 2001, New Mexico

Cross the street at night wearing dark clothing, and you court danger. Ride a push scooter down the center lane of a major road wearing dark clothes in the middle of the night, and you take your life into your hands. Ride that scooter in the dark carrying a bottle of Tequila Rose liqueur, and you're a Darwin Award waiting to happen.

An unidentified eighteen-year-old died doing just that, when the driver of a pickup truck veered to avoid his scooter and accidentally clipped him with the side mirror. The unhelmeted rider hit the pavement and died at the scene from severe head injuries.

In an earnest speech encouraging the use of common sense, Police Sergeant Brian McCutcheon warned that piloting a scooter down a street after dark is "a very bad idea" and "extremely unsafe."

Reference: *Albuquerque Journal*

Another deadly encounter with fate: Crystal Daze, page 17

DARWIN AWARD: CIRCULAR REASONING

Confirmed by Darwin

1998, LONDON

Two twenty-eight-year-old construction workers, reportedly experienced in their work, fell one hundred feet after cutting a hole through thick concrete without realizing they were standing in the center of the circle. Neither was wearing a safety harness to arrest his eight-story plunge.

Reference: The *Times* of London

A HAUNTINGLY SIMILAR STORY: Tied to His Work, page 100

**Darwin Awards: Where the ignorant
meet their logical conclusions.**

Darwin Award: Sweet Release

Confirmed by Darwin

1 January 2001, Illinois

Ralph and his fellow security officer were good friends who often relaxed together after work, while enjoying unusual games they had invented to relieve their frustrations. They called their games Sweet Release, Sixty-Five Percent Disability, and Million-Dollar Wound.

On New Year's Eve, Ralph's partner handed over his Glock semiautomatic handgun, saying, "Sweet release." The two men had exchanged duty weapons in their games on prior occasions, but this night ended differently. "I wonder if this is loaded." With those portentous parting words, Ralph stuck the gun in his mouth and played his final round of Sweet Release.

Investigators interviewed the two men and three women present during the fatal shooting, and all agreed that Ralph was his normal, happy self, and did not intend to commit suicide.

> Was this really Ralph's fault, or did he have an understandable expectation that his partner would not hand him a loaded gun? The jury's still out.

Although Ralph had been drinking with friends for several hours on the night of the accident, his blood alcohol level at 0.09 percent was barely over the state's legal limit for driving. This level is high enough to dull reflexes, but is not sufficient to seriously impair cognitive function.

The deceased had worked for the Charleston Police Department and the Champaign County sheriff's office before taking his

last job in security. But in all his years in law enforcement, he had apparently never fully absorbed the cardinal rule of handling weapons. Investigator Jim Rein explained, "Whether civilian or police officer, the assumption [should be] that every weapon is loaded."

Reference: *Champaign-Urbana News-Gazette*

SMARTER POLICE OFFICERS: The Sting, page 161

And the winner is . . . eliminated!

DARWIN AWARD: SNOWBALL'S CHANCE IN HELL

Unconfirmed by Darwin

5 MARCH 2001, DELAWARE

Two I-95 toll collectors were involved in a friendly snowball fight when one reached out to scoop some snow from a passing tractor-trailer rig. Manning a tollbooth is not the most interesting job, so it's only natural that collectors would engage in some freestyle entertainment. But scooping snow from a moving vehicle is not the safest of sports. The toll collector's hand caught in the rig, and he was pulled from his booth and dragged to his death.

Reference: *USA Today*

MORE GOOFING AROUND ON THE JOB: Instant Sunrise, page 145

DARWIN AWARD: SAND SURFING

Confirmed by Darwin

25 NOVEMBER 2000, AUSTRALIA

At the Spring Nationals country festival in Shepparton, a celebration truck drove noisily down Main Street at a sedate pace of five miles per hour, with frolicking people climbing all over it. The sight of the slow-moving truck gave a visitor from Cranbourne a bright idea. He decided to surf along behind it.

All decked out in his big Mexican hat, with a can of beer in one hand and a rope attached to the back of the truck in the other, he slid along the surface of the road on a piece of cardboard having a wonderful time . . . until the rope caught beneath the truck, and he was pulled under the wheels.

As if becoming a human speed bump weren't droll enough, the photo on the front page of the newspaper showed the corpse in a body bag—with the Mexican hat beside it!

ANOTHER INEBRIATED CELEBRATION: Fireworks Fiasco, page 132

HONORABLE MENTION:
HOUSE HUNTING GONE AWRY

Unconfirmed by Darwin
FEBRUARY 1995

Several men were contracted to move a house about five hundred yards, a short distance which nevertheless passed beneath several power lines that were roughly the same height as the house.

These quick-thinking men decided that one worker would ride on top of the house and use a board to lift the power lines over. Since the house was only traveling a short distance, and at a low speed, this plan seemed to be foolproof.

As you might guess, as soon as the damp pine board came in contact with the seventy-two-hundred-volt power line, the electricity raced down it, and the man was thrown from the top of the house. A coworker quickly extinguished his burning shirt and called for an ambulance.

The injured man was hospitalized with third- and fourth-degree burns to eight percent of his body. All of these idiots survived, so nobody can be nominated for a Darwin Award.

ANOTHER STORY ABOUT ELECTRICITY: Electrifying Stunt, page 66

First-degree burn: Damage is limited to the epidermis (skin), causing redness and pain. *Second-degree burn:* The epidermis and part of the dermis are damaged, producing blisters and mild to moderate swelling and pain. *Third-degree burn:* The epidermis and dermis are damaged. No blisters appear, but white, brown, or black tissue and damaged vessels are visible. *Fourth-degree burn:* The burn extends through deeply charred subcutaneous tissue to muscle and bone.

HONORABLE MENTION:
COORS LIGHT AND THE ULTRALIGHT

Confirmed by Darwin

13 SEPTEMBER 2000, INDIANA

The antics of an unidentified Lafayette pilot are surely a source of private chagrin to his relatives. During his fly-by-night escapades, the jovial aviator enjoyed circling an area of town and toasting the people below with Coors beer. One afternoon he went too far.

He was flying his UltraLight aircraft over a small subdivision of houses, saluting the spectators with his beer can, when he smashed into a homeowner's huge TV tower. It is a mystery how he could fail to notice the 150-foot structure, particularly as it was topped with a gaudy Christmas tree star, but fail to notice it he did. The aircraft knocked a forty-five-foot section out of the tower, sliced through three steel cables, and dove to within forty feet of the ground before the embarrassed pilot managed to regain control and fly away.

The Red Baron caused about $4,000 of damage. Although his identity is unknown, several clues were found at the scene: his left shoe, sunglasses, and a can of Coors Light were among the debris left behind. A compass and speedometer were also found. Police were baffled by the crash, and not sure whether to consider criminal charges. Lt. Rick Blacker said, "I don't think an UltraLight would classify as a vehicle."

The next time you are in Indiana, look for a guy with only one shoe and holding a beer. He just might be the mystery marauder.

Reference: lafayettejc.com

ANOTHER STORY INVOLVING BEER: Brewery Mishap, page 55

URBAN LEGEND: MAD TROMBONIST
AUGUST 1998, LATIN AMERICA

In a misplaced moment of inspiration, Enrique Medolino, bass-trombonist with a local orchestra, decided to make his own contribution to the cannon shots fired during a performance of Tchaikovsky's "1812 Overture" at an outdoor children's concert.

In complete disregard of decorum, he dropped a large lit firecracker, equivalent in strength to a quarter stick of dynamite, into his aluminum straight mute, and then stuck the mute into the bell of his new Yamaha in-line double-valve bass trombone.

Later from his hospital bed he explained to a reporter through a mask of bandages, "I thought the bell of my trombone would shield me from the explosion and focus the energy of the blast outwards and away from me, propelling the mute high above the orchestra like a rocket."

However Enrique was not up to speed on his propulsion physics, nor was he qualified to wield high-powered artillery. Despite his haste to raise the horn before the firecracker exploded, he failed to lift the bell high enough for the airborne mute's arc to clear the orchestra. What happened should serve as a lesson to us all during our own delirious moments of divine inspiration.

First, because he failed to sufficiently elevate the bell of his horn, the blast propelled the mute between rows of musicians in the woodwind and viola section, entirely bypassing the players, and rammed straight into the stomach of the conductor, driving him backward off the podium and into the front row of the audience.

Fortunately, the audience was sitting in folding chairs and thus protected from serious injury. The chairs collapsed under the first row, and passed the energy from the impact of the flying

conductor backward into the people sitting behind them, who in turn were driven back into the people in the third row, and so on, like a series of dominoes. The sound of collapsing wooden chairs and grunts of people falling on their behinds increased geometrically, adding to the overall commotion of cannons and brass playing the closing measures of the overture.

Meanwhile, unplanned audience choreography notwith-standing, Enrique Medolino's own personal Waterloo was still unfolding back on stage. According to Enrique, "As I heard the sound of the firecracker blast, time seemed to stand still. Right before I lost consciousness, I heard an Austrian-accented voice say, "Fur every akshon zer iz un eekval unt opposeet reakshon!"

This comes as no surprise, for Enrique was about to become a textbook demonstration of this fundamental law of physics. Having failed to plug the lead pipe of his trombone, he paved the way for the energy of the blast to jet a superheated plume of gas backward through the mouthpiece, which slammed into his face like the hand of fate, burning his lips and skin and knocking him mercifully unconscious.

But the pyrotechnic ballet wasn't over yet. The force of the blast was so great it split the bell of his shiny new Yamaha trombone right down the middle, turning it inside out while pro-pelling Enrique backward off the riser. For the grand finale, as Enrique fell to the ground, his limp hands lost their grip on the slide of the trombone, allowing the pressure of the hot gases to propel the slide like a golden spear into the head of the third clarinetist, knocking him senseless.

The moral of the story? The next time a trombonist hollers "Watch this!" you'd better duck!

𝄢 ANOTHER UNLUCKY MUSICIAN: Guitars 'n' Guns, page 134

PERSONAL ACCOUNT: ROBOT REAPER

Back in the early eighties a company that produced nuts and bolts decided to get ahead of the game and automate their warehousing. They installed a robot, which was basically a computer-controlled forklift that stored and retrieved bins of inventory. It had no eyes or other sensors to tell if somebody was in its path, and since it traveled twenty-five miles per hour, it was fairly dangerous.

The people who designed the system did not want a killer robot on their hands, so they enclosed the entire warehouse in a high barbed wire fence. They put a large "dead zone" around it with wide red stripes and painted DANGER signs on the ground. The gate was designed to stop the robot dead in its tracks the moment it was opened. It was also impossible to close it again from the inside.

Foolproof? No! Fools are so ingenious.

Our hero worked for this company, and needed a couple of bolts from the warehouse. Instead of going through normal procedures, he decided to save time and get them himself. He also felt that it was important not to interrupt the robot on its appointed rounds, though we will never know why.

Whatever the reason, he went to some trouble to set up a rope-and-pulley contraption that allowed him to close the warehouse gate from the inside. After thus ensuring that the robot was still operating, he tried to fetch himself some bolts, but instead earned a Darwin as the robot ran him down.

Reference: William D. Herndon, personal account.

ANOTHER MISADVENTURE RESULTING IN A LAWSUIT: Dive to Death, page 50

PERSONAL ACCOUNT: PROP ARC SAFETY
2001

Ten years ago I was an enlisted naval air crewman working in the turbo-prop-driven aircraft P-3 community. I remember a safety standdown story that was a favorite of us all.

As with every type of aircraft, there are safety zones to observe around a P-3, particularly in the vicinity of the props. Under no circumstances are you to walk through a prop arc, whether the plane is alive or dead.

During a late night preflight check, one flight engineer was on his visual walkaround when he walked right through a spinning prop untouched! He instantly realized what he had done and reflexively did a 180-degree turn right back into the prop, and was killed.

Many witnesses supposedly saw his expression the instant he turned around . . .

Reference: Anonymous personal account; NATOPS safety mishaps.

ANOTHER PLANE FLIGHT OF FANCY: Coors Light and the UltraLight, page 76

Of course this story isn't true. Props rotate at 500 to 600 rpm. Even a prop idling at a leisurely 200 rpm would make a full rotation every 0.3 seconds. If a prop has four blades, a fresh blade swings past a given point every 0.075 seconds. A man moving 4 mph moves about 70 inches/second. So in the interval between blade strokes, the man would move forward about 5 inches. Unless his head is less than five inches thick from the tip of his nose to the back of his skull, the next blade is going to hit him. Even slow prop speed, a fast pace, and perfect timing would not make this safety standdown story possible.

Personal Account: Miracle Mile
2001, Florida

A stretch of road in Clearwater dubbed the "Miracle Mile" carries three times its designed load of traffic. A few years ago I was approaching a green light at a busy intersection on the Miracle Mile when I noticed a fire engine, lights flashing and sirens blaring, trying to cross against the light.

People were whizzing by, oblivious to the fire engine, and preventing it from crossing. I don't know how they overlooked it—presumably they just chose to ignore it. If an emergency vehicle were responding to something involving me, I'd want it to have nothing but clear road, so I always give way.

I pulled up to the crosswalk and stopped, despite the green light. Traffic continued to whiz past me on both sides, ignoring the fire engine sitting at the intersection awash with lights and sirens. A guy in a white Lexus nearly rear-ended me, and as he gingerly nosed his way back into the traffic that was whizzing by, he locked eyes with me and gave me a single finger salute, holding eye contact until he was completely past me.

He faced forward just in time to see the fire engine smack in front of him. It had finally fought its way into the middle of the intersection. I'd have liked to stay and witness his ignominy, but instead I waved cheerfully and drove off, leaving him to explain to police and a dozen unhappy firemen how he could miss a forty-foot bright yellow fire truck with a shrieking siren and enough lights to outshine a Christmas tree.

Unfortunately, he didn't quite win a Darwin Award.

Reference: Alan Petrillo, personal account.

Another vehicle meets a bad end: Dog and Jeep, page 210
More unhappy firemen: Fifteen Minutes of Flame, page 137

CHAPTER 5

Men:

Male-functions

An insult to monkeys?

Darwinian Man, though well-behaved,
at best is but a monkey shaved.

— Gilbert and Sullivan's *Princess Ida* opera

Men suffer more than most from their own personalities and natural inclinations. Here's hoping the desire to shoot arrows, show off to young women, aim flying kicks, and accept ludicrous dares—become a bit less common someday.

Discussion: Online Safety

The communication medium of the Internet hides dangers along with its benefits. Like most technological advances, the benefits greatly outweigh the risks, but those who fail to use common sense may find that the reverse is true. Surfers are evolving mechanisms to protect themselves online.

To be safe, you should assess your comfort with public exposure, and understand the ramifications of information revealed and hidden while surfing the Internet. Are you a beautiful young woman, or can you act like one? You might find an online sweetheart at your door with a ring or a gun if you don't take steps to protect your privacy. Do you post inflammatory calls to violence in anarchic chatrooms and make catty comments about your management on message boards? You might get a pink slip and a subpoena if you don't guard your anonymity.

Even the readers of the Darwin Awards, more savvy than most from their aggregate decades online, are not immune from making foolish mistakes. Readers asked to prove they were adults "by their community's standards" in order to view sensitive photographs sent me credit card numbers, scans of licenses and passports, Social Security numbers, and photographs. I could have fled the country with ill-gotten wealth undreamt!

I met my partner on the Internet, an incomparable place to converse with people on a deep level. But I was also stalked by a man I'll call Hawk, who tracked me down to what he thought was my home in Las Vegas—only it was not me, but some other unfortunate Wendy. It is alarming to be chased on the Internet, and even more so when it splashes into real life. Keeping personal information private is an essential component of using the Internet safely.

Perhaps information was sent by children sneaking items from parents' wallets to "prove" their age. It's more hopeful to think that our children are that clever than to think that we are that stupid. But the more likely culprits are inexperienced Internet newcomers. The primary Internet safety rule is to not trust a stranger with information you wouldn't reveal to your rebellious teenage son. Next time you see a request for proof of age, know that all that's expected is the simple declaration, "I'm old enough to see the photos, so please send the URL."

Online safety is more than a matter of keeping your credit cards secret. It's also good practice to keep your name and whereabouts confidential unless you have a compelling reason to divulge them. One may choose to reveal information about oneself—what harm is done if the online bridge club knows your name is Denny? It's natural to reveal your wife, Caroline, works for Hewlett Packard, and that you eat at Meme's every Friday... and not realize that you've given potential stalkers all they need to track you down.

Sometimes information about you is available without your knowledge. Most Internet services assign an identifying number that discloses your city or even your neighboorhood. Some email addresses, particularly within the educational system, identify your name and location. Advertising cookies can track you from one website to another and cross-reference sets of registration information you provide to determine your identity.

Those new to the Internet, like children new to the world, are far more likely to fall prey to scam artists. As one spends more time online, one learns to avoid menace just as a child learns to safely navigate the physical world. Internet veterans speed the evolutionary process by sharing information and cautionary tales with "newbies," acting as teachers for new generations of students and speeding the evolutionary process.

Be open and trusting online, but only to a point. Be honest about yourself and your feelings so you can develop rewarding relationships, but be alert for deception and don't assume good intentions just because a person writes fluid email. Don't share your name, photograph, or identifying birthmarks without good reason. Obtain an anonymous email account, and consider using an "anonymizer" tool for added security. Never provide personal information without a good reason.

That's good sense on and offline.

See what you reveal about yourself.
www.DarwinAwards.com/book/showdata.html

Learn from the experience of others.
www.DarwinAwards.com/book/safety.html

The Internet with all its dangers is nevertheless a safer place than the physical world. The following stories prove that you should guard your life as vigilantly as you guard your on-line safety.

DARWIN AWARD: RAPPIN' ON HEAVEN'S DOOR
Confirmed by Darwin
28 FEBRUARY 2000, OHIO

Some artists bleed for their creative work, but usually not literally. That standard changed when a gangster-rap video artist put his final effort into his project and shot himself in the head while the cameras rolled.

Twenty-four-year-old Robert was creating the ten-minute video at his apartment with two colleagues. On camera, Robert reached for a .22-caliber handgun, swung the muzzle of the gun to his temple, and fired the gun.

Police were summoned to the scene by complaints from a neighbor who objected to the loud music and violent shouting. Robert died in a coma at the Ohio State University Medical Center.

Reference: *Columbus Dispatch;* WBNS Channel 10 in Columbus, Ohio
ANOTHER VIDEOTAPED FIASCO: Forklift Safety Video, page 65
MORE MUSICAL MISADVENTURES: Mad Trombonist, page 77

DARWIN AWARD: FANTASTIC PLASTIC LOVER
Unconfirmed by Darwin
NOVEMBER 2000, ENGLAND

A husband who frequently asked his wife to cover his nose and mouth with her nightie during lovemaking decided to add a plastic bag to his repertoire of solo sex tools. Martin, thirty-four, pulled a plastic bag over his head and used a vacuum cleaner to remove the air. He was found lying by the still-running vacuum cleaner, fully clothed, and very dead.

Reference: www.the-sun.co.uk
ANOTHER MAN WITH AN UNUSUAL YEN: Mad Trombonist, page 77

Robert, thirty-seven, shot himself dead while explaining gun safety to his wife. He placed a forty-five-caliber pistol he thought was unloaded under his chin and pulled the trigger. Robert's wife told police that the incident occurred after her complaints about her husband's extensive gun collection prompted him to demonstrate their safety.

(Darwin Award nomination of unknown veracity,
culled from a decade of email.)

Darwin Award: Bulletproof?

Unconfirmed by Darwin
March 2001, Ghana

Tribal clashes are common in Northern Ghana, and people often resort to witchcraft in the hope of becoming invulnerable to weapons. Aleobiga, twenty-three, and fifteen fellow believers purchased a potion that would render them invincible to bullets.

After smearing the magical lotion over their bodies for two weeks, Aleobiga volunteered to test the spell. The more prudent among us would at least test a non-essential body part for invulnerability, but not our hero. He stood in a clearing while his friends raised their weapons, aimed, fired . . .

The jujuman who had supplied the defective magic was seized and beaten for his failure, and Aleobiga is now roaming the great savanna in the sky.

Reference: Reuters

Another group with unrealistic expectations: All Aboard, page 53

**Darwin Awards:
Natural Deselection**

DARWIN AWARD: NEW DATING TECHNIQUE

Confirmed by Darwin

30 DECEMBER 1997, MEXICO

A security guard intending to impress female friends took a deadly gamble, losing his game of Russian roulette at a La Paz fast-food restaurant. Police say Victor, twenty-one, died instantly Saturday when he put his .38-caliber revolver to his head and pulled the trigger at a suburban hamburger outlet. Victor was trying to "impress some female friends," according to newspaper reports. The ladies were not available for comment, but one presumes that they were underwhelmed.

Reference: *Hoy de la Paz*

ANOTHER DEADLY PUBLIC ACT: Settle the Score, page 92

**Sperm: To be the fastest
does not mean you're the smartest.**

DARWIN AWARD: GOD SAVES?

Unconfirmed by Darwin

24 FEBRUARY 2001, IOWA

A wealth of literature makes it abundantly clear that deities often intercede to protect their sanctuaries from desecration. In light of this knowledge, a teenager who planned to burgle a church probably should have brought along his rosary and his cross.

David, sixteen, was on the roof of Grace Church in Des Moines lowering a stolen generator to the ground when his jacket became wrapped in the electrical cord, pulling him over the ledge to dangle precariously in the air. At that point he could have cut himself free with the sharp knife in his pocket or escaped by wriggling out of his jacket. Inexplicably, he did neither.

David died of exposure, trapped in the freezing rain. Next time you steal from a church, remember David's fate and reconsider. That bit of booty is not worth risking the wrath of a vengeful God.

Reference: *Des Moines Register*

ANOTHER INSTANCE OF GOD MOVING IN MYSTERIOUS WAYS:
Testing Faith, page 33

DARWIN AWARD: SETTLE THE SCORE

Confirmed by Darwin

4 JULY 2000, ALBERTA, CANADA

Yet another man has mistakenly shot himself in the groin, greatly reducing his chance of contributing to the gene pool. This particular example of a common miscalculation happened at a billiards room in Calgary.

The thirty-four-year-old man had been involved in an argument at 4 A.M., and came back to "settle the score," according to Calgary Police Inspector John Middleton-Hope. "[As] he pulled a small-caliber handgun from his waistband . . . it discharged."

The injured shooter, described by his wife as distraught, was taken to a hospital for treatment. His injuries weren't life threatening, "but I would suggest they were life-altering," said the inspector.

Reference: *Calgary Herald*

ANOTHER PAINFUL LESSON ABOUT GUNS: **Doggone Foot, page 117**

A twenty-three-year-old bar-brawler who had been bounced out of the Turtle Club in Florida sneaked back in and leaped off a staircase, aiming a kick at another man, and was killed when he landed on his head.

(Darwin Award nomination of unknown veracity, culled from a decade of email.)

DARWIN AWARD: HARDHEADS

Confirmed by Darwin

JANUARY 2001, AUSTRALIA

A thirty-seven-year-old man was enjoying the night air with his buddy, watching the stars overhead, feeling the Land Cruiser rocking gently beneath·him. . . Yes, he was riding *on top* of the vehicle, staring at the stars, relaxing during a ride home. An unexpected jolt, common on Australia's roadways, gave Dean a closer look at the stars as he was flung from the roof of the sports utility vehicle. Police said, "The deceased had been drinking, but what he was doing [lying] on the roof I'm not sure."

29 SEPTEMBER 2000, SOUTH CAROLINA

A thirty-two-year-old man hitching a ride on a pallet truck died when the vehicle passed under a bridge at fifty-five miles per hour and the concrete overpass struck the man's head. The driver told police that he had warned the riders not to sit up there but they were "hardheaded" and wouldn't listen.

Apparently the deceased wasn't hardheaded enough!

Reference: *Charleston Post and Courier, Courier-Mail of Australia*
 ANOTHER FELLOW WHO LOSES HIS HEAD: **Prop Arc Safety, page 80**

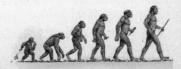

DARWIN AWARD: UR-INATE-IOT
Confirmed by Darwin
2 AUGUST 1999, WASHINGTON

In the small hours of the night, a nineteen-year-old male was uri-
nating off the freeway overpass on Pine Street when he lost his
footing and fell approximately forty-five feet to his death.

Was it torque?

Reference: Seattle Police Incident Report

ANOTHER CIRCUMSTANCE IN WHICH A PENIS CAUSED TROUBLE:
Horsing Around, page 123

**Reincarnation:
Lets you keep trying
until you get it right!**

DARWIN AWARD: A FELL DEATH

Confirmed by Darwin

22 FEBRUARY 2000, PENNSYLVANIA

A man clearing timber from his lot in Chestnuthill Township failed to notice that the tree he was working on had other trees leaning against it. When the weight of its neighbors pushed the tree over in his direction, the erstwhile lumberjack ran for his life, but slipped in the icy snow and fell directly in the path of the looming trunk, which landed on him with the expected result.

Reference: *Pocono Record*

ANOTHER DEADLY CONIFER: Christmas Tree, page 32

HONORABLE MENTION: CHEEZ WHIZ

Confirmed by Darwin

22 MAY 2000, ENGLAND

Every year Britons chase Double Gloucester cheese wheels down Cooper's Hill in an astoundingly bizarre and dangerous competition. Several seven-pound cheeses are hurled down the hill and dozens of contestants take off in pursuit. Their reward? If they catch a cheese, they get to keep it.

But Cooper's Hill is so steep that the cheese chasers invariably tumble as far as they run. This year was no exception. The "winner" broke his arm, yet managed to smile triumphantly while confessing that he had broken his other arm several years ago in a previous winning dash.

At least eighteen people were injured, including a spectator who tried to dodge a bouncing cheese. He was hospitalized for a head injury after a hundred-foot tumble down the steep slope.

Despite its bloody track record, the Gloucestershire tradition has continued for hundreds of years, and contestants show no signs of slowing down. They earn an Honorable Mention, and we fondly anticipate a cheese-chasing Darwin Award nominee in the near future.

See the cheese rolling movie!
www.DarwinAwards.com/book/cheese.html

Another dangerous English tradition in Ottery St. Mary, involves teams running through the town carrying burning barrels on their shoulders. Carrying a flaming barrel is dangerous, but so is gawking. Onlookers have been burned, trampled, and pushed through shop windows while trying to evade the bloke with the barrel.

Reference: Cable News Network, Reuters

ANOTHER UNLIKELY SPORTING EVENT: Sand Surfing, page 74

"Dumber than a bag of hammers."
"Stupider than a box of rocks."
"One sandwich short of a picnic."

HONORABLE MENTION: TRASH COMPACTOR

Confirmed by Darwin

8 MAY 2001, CANADA

Yet another unfortunate man has learned that sleeping in a Dumpster is far less attractive than it sounds. A thirty-six-year-old Saskatchewan man was dumped from his aromatic nest into a compactor and taken to a landfill, where his soft moaning alerted workers to his plight. Police and firefighters rescued him from the pile of garbage, and he was taken to a hospital and treated for a fractured jaw, arm, and ribs.

"I'm amazed he survived. They usually don't come out alive," said a spokesperson for Canada Waste Services. The compressor reduces loads to one-fifth their original size. "It's a four-meter drop onto a steel floor and then you are squeezed…"

Reference: South African Press Association, news24.co.za

MORE POOR CHOICES FOR A GOOD REST: Sleepfalling, page 18

A fool and his life are soon parted.

HONORABLE MENTION: ARCHERY PRACTICE

Unconfirmed by Darwin

9 OCTOBER 2000, CANADA

A young man was brought into a Toronto hospital with an arrow through his brain. The police explained that the victim had been practicing with a friend at an archery range and lost an expensive arrow by overshooting the target. The bowman searched the thicket behind the target, but couldn't find his arrow. So he called out to his friend, "Hey, shoot another one," thinking it would help him locate the original. The friend complied and the arrow flew true, striking the victim between the eyeballs and piercing his brain case. When last heard from, he was in intensive care with survival uncertain.

ANOTHER INSTANCE OF OVER-RELIANCE ON A FRIEND: Sweet Release, page 71

HONORABLE MENTION: TIED TO HIS WORK
Unconfirmed by Darwin
26 JANUARY 2001, FLORIDA

A twenty-four-year-old construction worker tied himself to a piece of scaffolding for safety while working on the fourth floor of the county jail annex. Forgetting he was attached to the metal, he tossed it to the ground . . . and was carried along for the ride. He landed on the scaffolding, which pierced both legs. He was treated for his injuries at Bayfront Medical Center in St. Petersburg and counseled on the use of his most important safety tool: his brain.

Reference: *Sarasota Herald-Tribune*

ANOTHER FALL FROM ANOTHER JAIL: Escaping Conviction, page 155

**It's not the fall that kills you,
it's the sudden deceleration.**

HONORABLE MENTION: CHICKEN WITH A TRAIN
Unconfirmed by Darwin

An Ohio student, nineteen, had his head bloodied when he was struck by a Conrail train. He told police he was trying to see how close to the moving train he could place his head without getting hit. Apparently his curiosity was stronger than his sense of survival.

MORE KIDS PLAYING WITH LARGE TRANSPORT: All Aboard, page 53
ANOTHER CONFRONTATION WITH A TRAIN: Killing Time, page 155

HONORABLE MENTION: TOILET TRAP

Confirmed by Darwin

31 JANUARY 2001, PENNSYLVANIA

A Huntingdon Valley man who dropped his keys in a portable toilet became stuck in the facilities while trying to rescue them. He hollered for help for forty-five minutes, until eventually children playing in a nearby field heard his cries and alerted their parents.

Police were forced to demolish the portable toilet to extricate the man, who had been standing in the redolent muck without his shoes or pants for an hour and a half. Doctors treated him for cuts and bruises, and removed the toilet seat wedged around his hips.

We speculate that his ego may never recover its original size.

Reference: *Gainesville (Florida) Sun*, Associated Press

ANOTHER EMBARRASSING STORY: Siphon!, page 166

URBAN LEGEND: THE BRICKLAYER

This accident report needs an introduction so you won't be lost at the beginning. This man was in an accident at work, so he filled out an insurance claim. The insurance company contacted him and asked for more information. This was his response:

"I am writing in response to your request for additional information for Block Number 3 of the accident reporting form. I put 'poor planning' as the cause of my accident. You said in your letter that I should explain more fully, so I trust the following details will be sufficient.

"I am an amateur radio operator and on the day of the accident, I was working alone on the top section of my new eighty-foot tower. When I had completed my work, I discovered that I had, over the course of several trips up the tower, brought up about three hundred pounds of tools and spare hardware. Rather than carry the now unneeded tools and material down by hand, I decided to lower the items down in a small barrel by using the pulley attached to the gin pole at the top of the tower.

"Securing the rope at ground level, I went to the top of the tower and loaded the tools and material into the barrel. Then I went back to the ground and untied the rope, holding it tightly to ensure a slow descent of the three hundred pounds of tools.

"You will note in Block Number 11 of the accident reporting form that I weigh only 155 pounds. Due to my surprise at being jerked off the ground so suddenly, I lost my presence of mind and forgot to let go of the rope.

"Needless to say, I proceeded at a rather rapid rate of speed up the side of the tower. In the vicinity of the forty-foot level, I met the barrel coming down. This explains my fractured skull and broken collarbone.

"Slowed only slightly, I continued my rapid ascent, not stopping until the fingers of my right hand were two knuckles deep into the pulley. Fortunately, by this time, I had regained my presence of mind and was able to hold on to the rope in spite of my pain. At approximately the same time, however, the barrel of tools hit the ground and the bottom fell out of the barrel.

"Devoid of the weight of the tools, the barrel now weighed approximately 20 pounds. I refer you again to my weight in Block Number 11. As you might imagine, I began a rapid descent down the side of the tower.

"In the vicinity of the forty-foot level, I met the barrel coming up. This accounts for the two fractured ankles, and the lacerations of my legs and lower body.

"The encounter with the barrel slowed me enough to lessen my injuries when I fell onto the pile of tools and, fortunately, only three vertebrae were cracked.

"I am sorry to report, however, that as I lay there on the tools, in pain, unable to stand and watching the empty barrel eighty feet above me, I again lost my presence of mind.

"I let go of the rope. . ."

Reference: Not a Darwin Awards contender since it is fiction, but too funny to exclude; submitted by "Dave" to the Yankee Clipper Contest Club and attributed to Gerald Hoffnung's "The Bricklayer" story, from his Oxford Union Speech, by an alert reader who goes on to say, "This bricklayer story has made the rounds on the Internet many times. Years ago it was on Garrison Keillor's radio show, and I also heard it verbatim on *Whadda Ya Know*. The story itself is quite a bit older. Many of our popular 'new' urban legends can be traced back several hundred years. People don't change much."

ANOTHER WORKMAN'S MISHAP: Circular Reasoning, page 70

PERSONAL ACCOUNT: TOURIST TRAP
DECEMBER 1997, FRANCE

A man who had been fascinated by the Roman Empire since he was a wee lad took off during a business trip to France to visit the ruins of an amphitheater and triumphal arch. He arrived in Avignon and settled in to read about them in a tourist's guide over dinner. He discovered that the famous aqueduct, constructed in the first century A.D. at Pont de Garde, was only twenty kilometers away.

It was a clear and windy night. Either under the influence of the full moon or a half bottle of Châteauneuf-du-Pape, or perhaps both, the history buff decided to drive out there after dinner and look around. He arrived to find the place deserted, with the road to the aqueduct chained off.

Under the light of the moon, he departed from the well-paved path of common sense, climbed over the chain, and ambled in for a closer look. As he approached the marvel of ancient engineering, gazing in what a charitable friend later called "childlike wonder" but others characterized as "an idiotic daze," the solid stone road seemed to fall out from under him.

What he had taken to be a shadow in the road was in fact a wide gap between the modern road and the aqueduct. He fell two meters to the bottom of a trench. Overhead, mocking his plight, hung the stone bridge where pedestrians are *supposed* to walk.

The trench could easily have been deep enough to prune his branch from the Tree of Life, but instead he escaped with a cracked rib and skinned shins, reminders of his painful lesson in reality.

Reference: Personal account by Jim Buchman, who hopes his daughter, Emma, is more levelheaded.

ANOTHER UNEXPECTED FALL: Fatal Footwear Fashion, page 36

Everyone starts off with a bag of luck and an empty bag of experience. The trick is to fill your experience bag before your luck is gone.

PERSONAL ACCOUNT: TUBE SNAKE
2001

A doctor in his final year of internship treated a slightly disheveled hippie lying on the examining table. His complaint was listed as "FBIP" which the nurse explained meant "Foreign Body In Penis." The patient's story was as interesting as one would expect, given his diagnostic acronym.

Several days previously he had been smoking marijuana when he decided to see what would happen if he snaked a three-foot length of aquarium tubing into his penis. He forced inch after inch into his urethra. When six inches still protruded, he tried to pull it out—but found that it was stuck!

This predicament apparently didn't teach him a lesson. He proceeded to thread a length of Weedwacker wire through the center of the tubing. The wire also became stuck. The patient decided to sleep on it and hope for the best.

The next day it was still stuck. He went about his gardening tasks as usual, hoping it would just fall out on its own, but the protruding tubing interfered with his chores, so he cut the tubing flush with his skin. Another day went by.

He finally concluded that, since the foreign objects were impeding the flow of urine, he needed to overcome his embarrassment and report to the nearest emergency room.

The doctor tugged on what little he could grasp of the tubing, but the patient was correct when he said it was stuck. X rays revealed that the tubing and Weedwacker wire were kinked and knotted in his bladder. A urologist was summoned to perform surgery, and using a scope forced through the patient's already-crowded urethra, he managed to cut the knots and pull out the tubing.

Needless to say, that is one stoned experiment the hippie will not try again.

Reference: Personal account by an anonymous M.D.

MORE MEN NEEDING MEDICAL INTERVENTION:
Men Eating Chili, page 22

Those without medical training find this doctor's lurid account difficult to swallow. A profusion of readers argue that the story is not possible, since catheters and other foreign materials cause great pain when inserted into the urethra, even under medical supervision. Despite their protests, the story is not so far-fetched. Many men do intubate themselves when required for urinary problems, such as those caused by an inflamed prostate gland. And medical literature confirms that sexual addicts gradually increase their pain tolerance to allow insertion of increasingly voluminous objects. Urologists collect stories of unlikely materials removed from awkward predicaments, and some even collect the items themselves.

Readers' comments on the story:
www.DarwinAwards.com/book/catheter.html

CHAPTER 6

Animals:
Pall of the Wild

*They've been treating these chimps
less than human.*
— Senator Mary Jane Garcia

*What separates man from other animals
is humanity.* —Senator Roman Maes
explaining his opposition to the death penalty

— both from the *Santa Fe New Mexican*

The call of the wild is heard less frequently in our
tame neighborhoods, but people still manage to get
in trouble with sheep, sharks, wasps, and lobsters.
Tales of wilderness woe remind us who's really in
charge of the earth.

Discussion: Dogs and Darwinism

Dogs are a species we have been breeding, and inbreeding, for 12,000 years. They are a study in genetic heritability. We find in dogs that you can selectively breed for:

- Physical traits (coat color and size).
- Personality (intelligent terriers, docile retrievers).
- Specific behaviors (herding dogs and guard dogs).

Dogs branched off from the wolves in the not-so-distant past. As we evolved from gatherers to farmers, we began to collect in settlements, and wolves collected on the borders. Animals that were particularly useful—for example those that brought killed game to the camp, or fetched slippers—were rewarded with scraps of food. Those that were dangerous were killed or driven away. People kept their favorite dogs alive through lean times. Thus an artificial selection was applied to the animals surrounding our villages.

We have taken the dog genome and selected for particular traits, and in doing so created dog breeds—inbred lines with less genetic diversity. Each dog breed represents a subset of the entire genome. Saint Bernards are large, muscular, and furry. Golden retrievers are golden brown, docile, and prone to spinal degeneration. Sheepdogs try to corral sheep, children, and grocery carts. One variety of guard dog barks when a stranger is a mile away, another when the stranger is twenty feet away. Guess which is quieter in your backyard!

A genetic defect common in large breeds of dogs provides an example of the dangers of limiting genetic diversity. Large purebred dogs such as German shepherds are prone to hip dysplasia, a degenerative nerve disorder that gradually paralyzes the spinal nerves beginning at the tail. Mongrel dogs occasionally come down with the disease as well, but far less frequently than susceptible breeds.

It is a small, inbred gene pool that sets the stage for a greater incidence of this dangerous genetic illness. Mongrels have more genetic diversity and fewer instances of the disease-causing allele than purebreds. Breeders are currently trying to reduce the incidence of hip dysplasia by not breeding those dogs suffering from this defect.

We also bred out traits such as aggression and violence. Today, dogcatchers and city restrictions on vicious dogs continue to eliminate dangerous behaviors. Put down a vicious animal, and you eliminate its vicious contribution to the dog genome. It is a community effort to limit the spread of dangerous dog genes—though, admittedly, dangerous dogs are often trained now rather than born as there is an unfortunate trend among a limited number of dog breeders to favor ferocious behavior in fighting dogs. But, overall, breeders select well-behaved dogs.

In short, our many dog breeds represent thousands of generations of genetic manipulation. Reshaping the dog genome—playing God with the dog—is a commonplace hubris that few question.

We learn from dogs that many canine personality traits are inherited, so surely human personality is also linked to the genome. We are born with the capacity for speech; other complex systems may well have a genetic basis. Might we also have innate confidence, ruthlessness, optimism, and a tendency to ignore authority? We haven't defined the full extent of genetic influence on personality, in humans or in animals.

Though we haven't defined the exact proportion of nature versus nurture when it comes to personality traits, most have a clear genetic component. How quickly we have selected for specific traits in dogs! If we wanted to, we could do the same for humans. Can you imagine breeding out violent aggression in man, as we do in dogs? Humankind condemns the notion, known as Social Darwinism, that humans can be selectively bred to become a better species. Our society forbids taking such ideas into the realm of reality, as happened during Hitler's abhorrent ethnic cleansing campaign.

We find similarly repugnant other practices which affect the gene pool. The unsavory idea that *Homo sapiens* murdered intelligent cousins in our rise to ascendancy reeks of selective breeding. And we have nearly universal prohibitions against incest and cannibalism. Our cultural taboos parallel our need for genetic diversity, thus the very ethical notions that we hold in such great regard may themselves be genetically determined!

An alternative view of dog evolution.
www.DarwinAwards.com/book/dog.html

The evil aspect of selective breeding lies in the imposition of the idea on unwilling victims. But most of us feel no particular grief when a person inflicts genetic improvement on *himself* by eliminating his genes through his own foolish actions. So enjoy the following Darwinian examples of self-selection— with animal assistance!

DARWIN AWARD: HORNET CHALLENGE
Confirmed by Darwin
27 JULY 2000, CAMBODIA

A motorcycle taxi driver in Phnom Penh challenged his neighbor to stand beneath a hornets' nest while two men pelted it with stones. The fifty-three-year old neighbor should have known better, but he had a local reputation as a "strong man" to uphold. He stood beneath the nest and the pelting commenced. The man endured the pain of countless stinging hornets before expiring from the toxic injections. Apparently he was not as strong as he thought.

Reference: Reuters, Rasmei Kampuchea

ANOTHER LOOK AT DANGEROUS ROCKS: Throwing Stones, page 16

The tree of life is self-pruning.

Darwin Award: Fish Gag
Unconfirmed by Darwin
1992, Zambia

A solo fishing expedition near Livingstone in Zambia turned into a tragedy when twenty-eight-year-old Harris was choked to death by a live fish that accidentally lodged in his throat. Harris hooked the fish from the Chungu River. When he tried to bite the fish to death, it slid down his throat. Harris tried to hook out the fish with a stick, but he pushed it farther down instead. The next morning, villagers going to the fields found his body sprawled on the ground with a stick dangling from his mouth. The fish came out when one of the villagers pulled on the stick.

Reference: *Hickory Daily Record*

Another choking mouthful: Morsel of Evidence, page 163

DARWIN AWARD: SHEEP SLEEP
Confirmed by Darwin
9 MARCH 2001, EGYPT

Police were baffled to discover a twenty-year-old Bedouin shepherd shot dead in the middle of the desert near Cairo. No one else was around, and no footprints led to or from the scene of the crime.

Investigators from Sidi Barrani sifted through the meager clues surrounding the death of the Bedouin, Mochtar, and soon fingered the culprit. The Egyptian man had fallen asleep amid his sheep without securing his rifle. One moment of neglect, one wooly misstep on the trigger, and a speeding slug sentenced the sleeping shepherd to his final slumber.

The unregistered weapon was confiscated from the flock, and the murderous sheep was sentenced to *ewethanasia*.

Reference: *Der Spiegel*, Reuters

ANOTHER UNHEALTHY SLEEPING ARRANGEMENT: Trash Compactor, page 98

Darwin Awards: Culling the Herd

HONORABLE MENTION: DOGGONE FOOT
Confirmed by Darwin
7 NOVEMBER 1999, FLORIDA

A Port St. John resident was never what neighbors would describe as friendly, so they greeted news of his recent self-inflicted wound with amusement. The man had been standing in his front yard aiming his gun at a neighbor's dog with malevolent intent. But his marksmanship proved lacking that day. When he squeezed the trigger, he hit his own foot instead of the mutt and wound up suffering in the hospital for his transgressions against man's best friend.

Reference: *Florida Today*

More rotten marksmanship: Archery Practice, page 99

Two animal rights activists were freeing a captive herd to protest the cruelty of sending pigs to a slaughterhouse in Bonn. Suddenly all two thousand of the pigs stampeded through the gate they were opening and trampled the hapless protesters to death.
(Darwin Award nomination of unknown veracity,
culled from a decade of email.)

URBAN LEGEND: CACTUS TALES
ARIZONA

A couple designed and built their own home, then headed for the Southwest on a combination vacation and home-decorating excursion. They filled a U-Haul truck with pottery and lawn ornaments, then headed for home.

On the way back, they camped at a tourist trap that sold potted saguaro cacti. They decided that one would fit perfectly into their front entryway, and blend nicely with their genuine Southwest decor. They chose a large specimen and added it to the load.

They arrived home and decorated their new house, and sure enough, the combination of unique architectural design and southwestern accents was eye-catching, especially the saguaro centerpiece.

Three weeks later they held a housewarming party.

As the party reached full swing, a fierce thunderstorm caused one of Arizona's frequent power outages. The experienced residents lit candles to push back the darkness, and forty jovial people continued to have a candlelight lark in the new home. The electrical lightning discharges were spectacular, so the candles were snuffed in order to enjoy the natural display.

Then someone screamed and pointed at the saguaro.

In the eerie lightning it had come to life, skin squirming and writhing. Several people turned their flashlights on the cactus and found that this was no mere trick of the light. The saguaro was moving!

The group fled to their cars, and neighbors summoned the police, who arrived promptly expecting to make a few hallucinogenic drug arrests. An animated cactus? They had barely cracked open the door of the house when they slammed it firmly shut again. Cops never moved so fast.

They taped off the house and called an exterminator. It turns out that tarantulas lay their eggs in trees and cacti along with small dead animals as food. The baby spiders are sealed in a hollow until their meal is gone, when they break out of their nursery and swarm the first living thing they find. They have been known to kill horses.

The saguaro the home decorators installed in their entryway had such a nest, and when the police opened the door they found the walls literally covered with baby tarantulas. The venom of the juvenile form is five times more potent than that of adults. If the homeowners had been asleep when the tarantulas ran out of food, they would have been swarmed and killed.

The moral of this story?

Do not bring the wild saguaro into your home!

ANOTHER SPIDERY CACTUS TALE . . .

The wife of a Marine stationed in Arizona was adjusting to living in the desert after the couple's recent transfer to the base. A gardening enthusiast, she went into the desert one day and dug up an attractive cactus for her home. Weeks passed, and the couple began to feel that something weird was going on with the cactus. It occasionally looked like it was undulating.

As time passed the movement became more discernible. Eventually they called a local plant expert and described the cactus and its unsettling behavior. The expert commanded them, "Leave the house immediately. Do not attempt to take any belongings. Just get out *now!*"

They ran outside in terror, and soon a group of exterminators arrived in biohazard suits and rushed into the house. The man and his wife watched through the window, and as they goggled at the cactus, it virtually exploded, unleashing thousands of tarantulas in the house.

ANOTHER DEADLY PRICKLE: Man and Cactus, page 142

And now an injection of reality! An Arizona Cactus & Succulent Research, Inc., spokesperson says, "These legends have been circulating for years. Neither is true. Tarantulas are not deadly, nor do they make their homes in cacti." Tarantulas live underground, and mothers lovingly tend egg cocoons the size and weight of a cotton ball, which is far too small to hatch into a cactus-moving brood. Baby tarantulas are not more venomous than adults, which in fact are not particularly toxic to humans. The tarantula legend is soundly debunked in *The Mexican Pet* by Jan Brunvand.

HONORABLE MENTION: POLAR BEAR LESSON
Confirmed by Darwin
SEPTEMBER 1994, ALASKA

Anchorage residents have seen it all now! Two inebriated teenagers decided to swim with polar bears in the Anchorage Zoo. They jumped over one fence and climbed through another to get to the pool, where Binky the Bear took immediate offense and mauled the first of the male intruders. The man's prostate suffered dearly for his mistake, but he survived. The second intruder escaped unscathed.

As an interesting footnote, a new pen was under consideration because the old one was much too elaborate for its purpose of keeping the polar bears inside. In light of this escapade, maybe they should emphasize making the pen difficult for people to get into, instead of worrying about the bears getting out.

References: Personal account by Tyler Thickstun and numerous media sources.

A reader who remembered Binky said, "The same year, an Australian tourist climbed into the cage to snap a picture. Binky came away from the experience with a sneaker, which he played with to the end of his days. A local fire department printed 'Bad as Binky' T-shirts with a drawing of Binky holding the sneaker in his mouth. Sadly Binky and his mate died within months of each other in the mid-nineties."

ANOTHER CASE OF ANIMALS GETTING EVEN: Revenge of the Gopher, page 203

PERSONAL ACCOUNT: FEEDING THE DOLPHINS

An active duty member of the United States Coast Guard, I was stationed in Florida in 1995. While on routine patrol I noticed a woman tossing baitfish around. She was standing in four feet of water, thirty meters from the beach. I thought she was feeding the dolphins, which is illegal in the state of Florida, so I pulled up alongside her to advise her of the infraction.

I looked down into the water and noticed that the tails on these creatures were moving from side to side, as opposed to up and down like a dolphin. And none were coming up for air. This misguided woman was hand-feeding a school of sharks!

Trying not to alarm her, I asked if she had noticed anything unusual. When she realized she was surrounded by ten sharks, her face turned white as a ghost and she jumped into my boat before I knew what had happened!

The guys back at the station had a good laugh over that one.

Reference: Gerald Martin, personal account.

ANOTHER BOAT ON THE WATER: Duct Tape, page 47

And we are the top of the food chain?

Personal Account: Horsing Around
2001

A man in his early thirties visited the emergency room of a small rural hospital in Ohio, but he refused to tell the nurse what was wrong. When a patient says it's "something private to discuss with the doctor," that usually indicates a tragedy or a comedy, and it's always interesting. This case was no exception.

When the doctor walked in with his chart, the man sheepishly unfastened his pants to reveal his injured penis. Fortunately it was not bleeding, but there was an appalling mid-shaft gash going at least halfway through. After the initial shock, the doctor peered closer and saw a few torn-out stitches.

The patient explained that the week-old injury had already been repaired by a urologist, and he had come into the emergency room merely because the wound had opened up again. Naturally the physician asked him how the injury had happened.

He said he had "tried to make a horse do something she didn't want to do," and been bitten in the process. He deserves a Darwin Award since the wound caused by his attempt at horse fellatio severed the nerves necessary to procreate, although he retained his (disfigured) penis.

Reference: Anonymous personal account.

Another odd sex habit: Fantastic Plastic Lover, page 88

URBAN LEGEND: LOBSTER VASECTOMY
2000

This tale proves that crime does pay, if you're fishing for elective surgery to go along with your stolen goods. A twenty-four-year-old supermarket shoplifter stuffed a pair of live lobsters in his pants and sprinted for the door, but he never had a chance. The violated crustaceans brought the thief to his knees in front of startled cashiers when they fastened their powerful claws around his delicate parts.

Doctors were able to remove the animals with pliers. They said the thief would fully recover—except for one small detail: "It was a do-it-yourself vasectomy." This man's daring supermarket exploits make him one of the few Darwin Award winners to live to tell the tale. The supermarket manager declined to press charges, saying the culprit had already "gone through enough pain to learn his lesson."

Reference: *Los Angeles Times, Key West Citizen*

I've labeled this story an Urban Legend, but I'm not sure about that. Perhaps it is true. Signs are against it. Florida lobsters have no large claw, astoundingly enough. In any case lobster claws are restrained with bands by the time they get to the supermarket, making this mishap unlikely. A urologist reader deemed the story medically implausible, as a force strong enough to sever the vas deferens, which would sterilize the victim, would almost certainly crush the blood vessels, thus requiring removal of the testes.

The jury's still out. What do you think?
www.DarwinAwards.com/book/lobster.html

A DIFFERENT KIND OF VASECTOMY: You Said a Mouthful, page 160

CHAPTER 7

Explosions:
Out with a Bang!

*It may be that your sole purpose in life
is simply to serve as a warning to others.*

— Unknown

Our fascination with incendiary devices is as old as
the first blazing firepit. Now that the campfire days
are gone, we may eventually lose our love of explosives . . . but we will undoubtedly lose a few limbs in
the process.

DISCUSSION: INTELLIGENT DESIGN THEORY

Religious critics of evolution champion creationism—the idea that a literal interpretation of the Bible offers a more accurate account of human origins than does Darwinian theory. A look at several once-fashionable arguments against evolution is both amusing and instructive.

The fossil record shows increasing complexity over time, which supports the idea of evolution. Creationists once claimed that the biblical Flood might have stratified fossils based on density, much like a sifter separates small particles from large. Thus an observed increase in complexity may have arisen from the Flood, rather than from evolution. While the idea of a massive flood is interesting speculation—recent research reveals molten hot spots circumnavigating Earth's core that transiently sink entire continents, thus explaining ancient sea beds on the mile-high Denver plateau—there is no real evidence to support the notion of flood-as-stratifier. And today geological dating techniques directly date fossils without relying on their physical organization.

An older and more naive argument against evolution was that new species cannot arise from existing species. "The horse and the donkey are bred to form a mule, but the mule is sterile. A lion and a tiger produce the sterile liger. Therefore new species cannot arise from existing species." As explained in the discussion on speciation, page 190, no one supposes new species are combinations of old species, so this is an outmoded objection to evolution.

Critics of Darwinism have been increasingly hard-pressed to support their objections. Enter Intelligent Design Theory, or IDT. This "theory" was brought to light not in a reputable scientific journal, but rather by a self-described "intelligent design think tank" in Washington called The Discovery Institute. They argue that extremely complex systems, such as those with multiple interrelated parts like the lens and retina of the eye, or wings and feathers, could not have arisen spontaneously—and therefore must be the result of a supernaturally powerful designer.

After all, a watch doesn't repair itself.

> *hypothesis* (n) A tentative explanation for an observation that can be tested by further investigation.
>
> *theory* (n) An explanation for a set of facts that has been repeatedly tested, is widely accepted, and can be used to make predictions about natural phenomena.

Irreducible complexity is the cornerstone of IDT. They are referring to complexity too mind-boggling to have been created from infrequent random genetic mutations shaped by the pull of natural selection over billions of years—features that are obviously irreducibly complex and thus cannot have occurred without intelligent intervention.

At what point does one decide that a feature is irreducibly complex, proving that an unimaginably intelligent designer in-

tervened? How do we know that human eyes, for example, are too complex to have evolved but for the intervention of an "intelligent designer"? Scientists can formulate persuasive explanations for the development of the eye, beginning as a light-sensitive patch of cells, but even the best attempt to explain any given complex system cannot *disprove* IDT.

The problem with the idea of irreducible complexity is that it is not testable. And the cornerstone of science is that a hypothesis *must be testable* in order to determine how well it fits the facts. Because there is no way to test IDT, it can never achieve acceptance as a scientific theory.

The idea of an intelligent designer is alluring to those who believe in a literal interpretation of theological texts. But IDT cannot compete with the theory of evolution, an explanation for the diversity of life that is supported by extensive probing from the scientific community, and the contents of a vast experimental knowledge base.

Because it is not testable, the latest version of creationism—Intelligent Design Theory—is anything but.

More on Intelligent Design Theory:
www.DarwinAwards.com/book/idt.html

Throughout history man has pondered the origins of life. Greek philosophers believed that all life is composed of four elements: earth, air, fire, and water. This chapter explores what happens when the elements become unbalanced, and fire is allowed to take the upper hand.

DARWIN AWARD: OUT WITH A BANG!

Confirmed by Darwin

19 APRIL 2000, GEORGIA

Robert, a mechanic at a Montezuma tire store, was killed when a tire on the wheel he was repairing exploded. He had been attempting to fix a crack in a tractor-trailer wheel rim with a welding torch. Any mechanic can tell you that heating air in a sealed container, such as a truck tire, causes the gas to expand and the pressure to increase. But the mechanic had been repairing tires for years and was too busy to deflate the tire before fixing the crack.

Witnesses say that when the four-foot-diameter tire exploded, the rim left the axle "with great velocity" and struck Robert in the head, killing him instantly. The force of the explosion was enough to knock a pickup truck off of a nearby lift, and the report was heard at the local police station one mile away.

The Occupational Safety and Health Administration cited and fined the tire and wheel company, but the owner says he will contest the findings. "He was trained. The manager and the customer told him not to, but he did it anyway."

Reference: *Macon Telegraph*

MORE MEN ENGAGED IN REPAIRS: Workin' on the Railroad, page 141

Why did the tire explode? There are multiple hypotheses. Montezuma Police Chief Lewis Cazenave theorized that heat from the welding torch caused the air in the tire to expand until it exploded. One reader protested that the air would not expand enough to actually burst the tire, and speculated that moisture inside the tire caused the explosion when it was heated to the boiling point. Other readers fingered flammable materials exuded from rubber and glue, or the presence of volatile gases such as butane or propane, commonly used in quick-fix tire repair kits. A knowledgeable mechanic opined that it may have been a split-rim. "Split-rims have a one-piece locking ring split to fit between the rim and the tire bead. These tires are placed in a protective cage when inflating, in case the ring slips. Exploding split-rims can punch holes through cinderblock walls." Though opinions differed, all agree that one should never weld on a wheel that is still attached to the tire.

DARWIN AWARD: GRENADE JUGGLER

Unconfirmed by Darwin

MAY 2001, CROATIA

A college student dropped the ball when a hand grenade exploded while he was juggling it at a party in Vidovci. Six students watching him were also injured.

A spectator is usually disqualified from winning a Darwin Award caused by another's idiocy, but this audience should have known better than to gape at a man juggling explosives. The six onlookers earn Honorable Mentions for their disregard of common sense, and the juggler wins a Darwin for his lethal stupidity.

Reference: *Sun*, England

ANOTHER SPORT DANGEROUS TO ONLOOKERS: Cheez Whiz, page 96

Famous Last Words:
"Safe? Of course it's safe!"
"I wonder what this button does?"
"I bet no one's ever done this be—"

DARWIN AWARD: FIREWORKS FIASCO

Confirmed by Darwin

4 JULY 2000, NEW YORK

America's Independence Day celebration is a festival for pyro-maniacs. People routinely lose fingers and eyes in fireworks explosions, year after year, seemingly oblivious to the dangers. And the bigger the fireworks, the greater the damage.

Keith, thirty-four, suffered partial decapitation when he peered into the mouth of a launching tube containing what he thought was a malfunctioning aerial firework.

The unlicensed pyrospectacular display was to be the grand finale of his party, and in his haste to correct the problem he placed his head directly over the opening. After a short delay the fireworks exploded, giving both his head and his party an impromptu yet spectacular grand finale.

Reference: Associated Press

ANOTHER PARTIAL DECAPITATION: Hardheads, page 93

**Making the human race smarter,
one idiot at a time.**

Darwin Award: Shell Shot

Unconfirmed by Darwin

20 October 1999, Texas

A twenty-one-year-old man died from shrapnel wounds when he and his friends discovered and began shooting at two explosive devices. The three men found the seventy-five-millimeter "ceremonial military rounds" while cleaning out a building, and someone decided it would be a worthy challenge to see if they could trigger the explosives with gunfire. You know what? It worked. One man died at the scene, and the remaining two stepped aside to let the Fort Hood Bomb Disposal Unit do their job.

Reference: KXXV-TV, Waco/Temple/Killeen, Texas

Twenty-one is a dangerous age: Stab in the Dark, page 159

Two soldiers died in their tent when fumes from an illegal propane heater snuffed their lives in Barstow, California. Officials said they were on a U.S. Army training exercise in the Mojave Desert when they broke new ground in misuse of gas-powered equipment.

(Darwin Award nomination of unknown veracity,
culled from a decade of email.)

DARWIN AWARD: GUITARS 'N' GUNS

Confirmed by Darwin

23 JANUARY 1978

Legendary Chicago guitarist Terry Kath was an avid collector of guns. One week before his thirty-second birthday, he brought several of his cold metal friends to a party along with his wife. After the party broke up, he began to play with his guns.

First he spun his .38-caliber revolver on his finger, brought it to his temple, and pulled the trigger. Click! The gun was not loaded. Next he picked up a 9mm semi-automatic pistol. The host of the party, unamused, asked him to stop. As Terry pulled the magazine from the weapon, he reassured him, "Don't worry it's not loaded." Then Terry raised the pistol . . . and put a bullet through his head in an one-man shootout.

This popular musician and longtime gun enthusiast forgot that an automatic automatically chambers a bullet, so removing the magazine does not disarm the weapon.

His death was classified an inadvertent suicide.

ANOTHER .38 SPECIAL: New Dating Technique, page 90

A few automatic weapons have a trigger lockout and will not fire without a magazine loaded, but the majority will fire with or without the magazine. Russian roulette just became a magnitude harder!

HONORABLE MENTION: KABOOM!

Confirmed by Darwin

14 JULY 1999, ARKANSAS

A mobile home in Little Rock was destroyed when a resident used a cigarette lighter to peer inside a gasoline can. It's the same old story: Marcel was trying to determine whether there was water in the gas can when he discovered that it contained . . . gas! The flammable fumes caught fire and Marcel slung the can onto the floor, splattering gasoline which ignited and set the residence ablaze. He suffered minor burns on his hand.

The homeowner and her son escaped the blaze, but the family dog did not survive.

Reference: CNN, *Los Angeles Times, Dallas Morning News,*
Associated Press, *New York Daily News*

MORE FUMES AFIRE: JATO, page 193

HONORABLE MENTION: PLANE STUPID
Unconfirmed by Darwin
5 FEBRUARY 1981, CALIFORNIA

Phoenix Field airport had been subject to recurring petty thefts from neighborhood teenagers, so a security firm was retained to patrol the grounds. Thefts decreased sharply, but fuel consumption was on the rise. This puzzling situation continued until late one night, when a passerby noticed a flaming airplane on the field.

By the time the fire department arrived, the plane had completely melted into the tarmac. While they extinguished the residual flames, the passerby noticed a uniformed figure lying facedown several yards away. It was a security guard!

He was revived and questioned.

Turns out he had been siphoning fuel from small planes to use in his car. The plane he selected that night had a unique fuel storage system involving hollow, baffled wing spars. When the determined guard shoved the siphon in, it stubbed against the first baffle. No matter how he twisted, pushed, and pulled the hose, he could not siphon any fuel from the plane.

Exasperated, he lit a match to see inside the tank . . . and the rest is history.

Reference: Submitted by David L. Baker, *Sacramento Bee*

⚘ A MORE VIRTUOUS SECURITY GUARD: Emergency Room Excitement, page 23

URBAN LEGEND: FIFTEEN MINUTES OF FLAME

Written as an April Fools' Day joke
1 APRIL 2001, NEW YORK

A literary agent found himself dazed and patting out flames shortly after arriving at a two-alarm house fire equipped with a sandwich, a bullhorn, whiskey, and a lawnchair. He climbed to the roof of a nearby house, perched on his lawnchair, and proceeded to lecture the startled emergency crew while enjoying his drink.

Three firemen had just finished clearing the house, locating the residents' young golden retriever in the process, when they heard the agent's imperious command. "Drop the dog and open the hydrant this instant!"

They turned in surprise and dropped the yelping puppy, which fell through the burning timbers and burst into flames. Onlookers mobbed the base of the heckler's house and threw cans and shrubbery at the obstreperous critic, who batted the projectiles aside with his bullhorn while continuing to drink whiskey and issue commands.

"The north side is engaged!"

"Position the hose along the azalea bushes!"

"Stop picking your nose!"

Sorely provoked, the senior fireman, currently on administrative leave, picked up the dead but still burning dog and flung it onto the roof. The flaming animal landed in the loudmouth's lap, igniting his spilled whiskey and severely burning his crotch.

He heaved the dog off, but neglected to brace his feet on the slanted roof. Man and lawnchair toppled and fell from the house, miraculously avoiding onlookers, who watched aghast while the prostrate man suffered further injuries from falling embers and his own rooftop accoutrements.

The house fire was eventually subdued, and paramedics transported the injured man and his bullhorn to the hospital. Although he is recovering from his injuries, the prognosis is that he will never again be able to procreate with quite the same gusto.

ANOTHER ENCOUNTER WITH FIRE: Brush with Stupidity, page 41
ANOTHER IGNOMINIOUS FALL: Ur-inate-iot, page 94

**Half of the people you know
are below average. Natural selection
is attempting to decrease that proportion.**

PERSONAL ACCOUNT: A MEDIEVAL TALE
1600s, HUNGARY

One of the oldest Hungarian legends takes place during the late medieval years. It may even be true.

Paks, today a small city boasting Hungary's single nuclear power plant, was a small village in the 1600s. Back then, the village endured an ongoing provocation from a neighboring village. They kept sending their cows to graze on Paks land—and vice-versa, if I know my ancestors.

Once a foreigner attacked a Paks herdsman, beat him badly, and confiscated his cows. But this was not just any herdsman, it was the son of the mayor! The people of Paks took up arms, or rather work tools they could wield as arms. The result was a small battle between the two villages, in which dozens of peasants bit the dust.

The brave Paks army retreated in defeat.

The mayor of Paks, undaunted, ordered his men to fabricate a cannon to blast the enemy to smithereens. It was easier to order it than to construct it, as they did not have the necessary tools and materials to build a cannon. "No matter," said the wise mayor. "Chop a tree down and create the cannon from its trunk!"

During the night the people of Paks created the first wooden cannon in history, ready for deployment. They towed it up a nearby hill, and the entire village gathered around to observe the victory.

The gunmaster loaded the cannon with gunpowder, put a large rock projectile in the barrel, pointed the weapon toward the enemy village, and fired it . . . KABOOM!

Twenty people near the cannon died, and many others were seriously wounded. The mayor, who was uninjured, immediately issued a victory proclamation for his people, declaring, "If we have so many dead, how many can be left of the enemy?"

Reference: Tamas Polgar, personal account.

ANOTHER BATTLEGROUND DELUSION: Bulletproof?, page 89

ANOTHER HISTORIC RUIN: Tourist Trap, page 105

**Learn from the mistakes of others.
You won't live long enough
to make them all yourself.**

PERSONAL ACCOUNT: WORKIN' ON THE RAILROAD
FEBRUARY 2001, VIRGINIA

Several years ago a brand-new locomotive was brought in for repair after it was involved in an accident. While the shop was fixing the fuel tank, a significant amount of diesel fuel spilled on the floor. The foreman assigned two shop laborers to clean up the fuel.

As they worked, the men began to argue about the flammability of diesel. One had seen a demonstration on the David Letterman show the previous night, in which a science teacher extinguished the host's cigar in a jar of diesel fuel. The man decided to demonstrate this principle to his coworker, but he was unable to find a cigar, so he climbed into the cab and retrieved a road flare. He struck the flare and threw it into the spilled fuel.

Unfortunately for all concerned, road flares burn much hotter than cigars, and the spill was not deep enough to submerge the burning end. The fuel ignited quite easily, and although the workers escaped injury, the locomotive was gutted and the repair facility suffered extensive damage.

Reference: Anonymous personal account.
MORE PROOF THAT FUMES AND FIRE DON'T MIX:
Explosive Mix of Girls, page 37

Flares contain both fuel and an oxidizer, thus they will burn even when immersed in liquid. A cigar contains only fuel, and readers assure me that it can indeed be extinguished by dunking it in diesel fuel—but not gasoline, because of its greater volatility. Call me skeptical—I'm not testing the theory!

PERSONAL ACCOUNT: MAN AND CACTUS

An experience with the instability of one saguaro cactus.

Years ago we were drinking beer in the desert of northern Mexico and entertaining ourselves by exploding crude locally made fireworks. They were large triangles of multilayered newspapers filled with some kind of explosive, with a fuse emanating from one corner. The explosions were satisfyingly loud.

One of us threw one of these explosive devices and it happened to land at the base of a saguaro, where it promptly exploded. This particular cactus, which was well over twelve feet tall and lined with heavy spikes, tumbled over and hit the desert floor.

Fortunately none of us were in its path.

Sources say you would need a stick of dynamite to knock one over—desert cacti have extensive root systems which not only collect and store every precious drop of water, but also anchor them strongly to the ground. The combination of hard desert clay and extensive roots anchors a cactus upright for its entire life, and years after its death.

Reference: Anonymous personal account.

AN URBAN LEGEND ABOUT A SAGUARO: Cactus Tales, page 118

PERSONAL ACCOUNT: MAN WITH GAS CAN
MARCH 2000, WEST VIRGINIA

Here's an episode that I had the pleasure of witnessing firsthand. I worked in a small engine repair shop in my hometown, where intelligent people are outnumbered by the dangerously ignorant.

One of these simpletons brought his rusty lawnmower in for repair. He was a suspicious person who suspected that we were out to rip him off. When he picked up his mower, he was prepared to start it up in our parking lot to make sure the job was done right.

I watched from the safety of the garage thirty feet away.

He took a gas can from the bed of his pickup and attempted to fill the gas tank. He had a lit cigarette dangling from his lip as he fumbled with the gas can. The tank's opening was very small, and he had no funnel or spout, so more gas poured on the ground than into the tank.

He decided to improvise with a Styrofoam cup, and things rapidly went from bad to worse. If you have ever seen gasoline and Styrofoam combine, you know that his wasn't a wise course of action. The cup disintegrated and emptied its contents on the man's pants.

He jumped back and dropped the gas can, which landed on its side and began to gurgle more gasoline down the gentle slope of the parking lot. The cigarette fell from his mouth, almost in slow motion, and a rush of adrenaline shot through me as I watched the gasoline ignite in a loud *poof*.

The fire climbed the man's legs and covered the parking lot and lawnmower. The flames raced toward the gas can and engulfed it. Luckily my boss had been watching as well, and lickety-split he was out the door with a fire extinguisher and, dousing the flames.

Paramedics took the idiot to the hospital, where he was treated for second-degree burns to his legs and hands.

Years later I heard he was killed working on the transmission of his truck while it was parked on a steep incline. The wheel blocks gave way, and the truck rolled over him.

Reference: Jocko Jones, personal account.

MORE FOLLY WITH FUEL: Plane Stupid, page 136

Nothing is foolproof to a sufficiently talented fool.

PERSONAL ACCOUNT: INSTANT SUNRISE
1980, MICHIGAN

The worst-case scenario was averted at the last second, but it was a close one. I was stationed at an air force base in Michigan which flew B-52 bombers. One of my jobs was to haul nuclear weapons from storage to the planes and back. We towed them on a bolster, a spindly cart with a caster on each corner, on which we perched four-megaton nuclear bombs.

In order to tow the bolster, you had to unlock either the front or the rear casters, but never both, and hook it to a truck.

One morning, I was assigned to work with a man I loathed—and the feeling was mutual. While I was inspecting the loaded bolster, I unlocked the front set of casters, not realizing that he had unlocked the rear set.

We weren't speaking to each other, you see.

The bolster rolled out of the building easily enough, but as soon as we made a tight turn, all four casters swiveled and I saw in the rearview mirror a sight I will never forget. The bolster was rolling majestically to the left, while the right-hand casters were canted eight inches off the ground.

When my coworker heard my terrified gasp, he slammed on the brakes—thus keeping the bolster from rolling completely over. He carefully put the vehicle into reverse and eased the bolster back down.

Would those four nuclear bombs have created an instant sunrise if they hit the ground? No! The safety precautions would prevent that. But each bomb carries a load of high explosive in the trigger mechanism, which certainly would have detonated, scattering radioactive material over the Michigan countryside, and turning me and my coworker into unpleasant memories.

Had the accident progressed to its logical conclusion, I believe we would have earned a Darwin entry with a half-life of several thousand years.

Reference: Anonymous personal account.
MORE MEN IN TROUBLE ON THE JOB: Out with a Bang!, page 129

Were these blundering bolster boys close to creating a nuclear incident in Michigan? Readers chimed in with opinions to the contrary.

DRHALL
The U.S. government would not allow a nuclear weapon to be transported by two people with no security. There would be dozens of men around this weapon.

GLR
Large U.S. weapons have safety features that prevent inadvertent explosions. For example, torpedoes and missiles must reach a minimum speed before the warhead will explode, and some nuclear weapons have four conventional explosives which must be triggered at precisely the same moment to detonate the warhead.

SMASHOGRE
Even conventional weapons have redundant safeties. Sidewinder missiles are rail launched, and not armed until the missile leaves the rail. Sparrow missiles have a tether attached to the arming mechanism, which pulls free when the missile is jetti-

soned. Some weapons have a front-mounted propeller which must count so many revolutions before the detonator is armed.

JAKE

I studied all accidents involving nuclear weapons in the fifties and sixties. These weapons are designed to survive an aircraft impact.

MY2CENTS

I owned eighteen of these golden bullets as a special weapons officer in Germany. This story is full of crap. They can roll on the ground, get shot, and even burn without exploding. The charges detonate only after receiving a unique electrical pulse.

THEXIA

I know from experience that accidentally dropping a nuke isn't rare in our military.

The author of this account responds, "When weapons are moved inside the storage area, as these were, two people are sufficient, as they are under surveillance from the watchtower or patrols at all times. And while a nuclear explosion wouldn't happen, my USAF Munitions Systems Specialist and Nuclear Weapons Decontamination training was unequivocal: if whacked hard enough, a conventional explosion *will* occur. In the late 1950s, a weapon accidently dropped from a B-47 landed in a farmer's yard, wrecking his house with the explosion."

Instant Sunrise: Fiasco or Fabrication?
www.DarwinAwards.com/book/sunrise.html

CHAPTER 8

Outlaws:
Crime and Punishment

I did not go to his funeral,
but I wrote a nice letter saying
I approved of it.

—Mark Twain

Living outside the law is a time-honored tradition, but an increasingly dangerous profession. College tuition is cheaper and more profitable than the cost these criminals bear to learn that crime does pay—in pain.

DISCUSSION: CITY LIVING

The stories in this chapter are about criminal misadventures. Crime is one of many significant dangers faced by city dwellers. Is it safe to live in a city?

All night long trucks carry supplies from fields and factories into our cities. Truckers sleep in their rigs by the side of the road, and wake to resume the never-ending journey, like industrious ants carrying goods from those who produce to those who consume. Transportation systems such as freeways allow large concentrations of consumers—otherwise known as cities—to live far from the sites of production.

What would happen if the transportation infrastructure were damaged?

Railroads can be blocked by landslides. Waterways can be embargoed by military force. Freeways can collapse in an earthquake or explosion. If key access routes were destroyed, all goods would have to arrive via a less efficient route, and local supplies would inevitably run low. Imagine meat and vegetables being conveyed hand-to-hand past the transit breakpoint. Would you have enough to eat and drink if disaster struck near you?

A city's population cannot survive without a constant influx of goods. Food reserves are generally sufficient for a few days, no more. Supplies would quickly run low, and the inhabitants would be left starving and scavenging the streets. Theft could well become the only viable means of survival for hungry people.

The chance of such a bleak scenario coming to pass is difficult to ascertain. It depends on the number of roadways and railways leading into a town, whether it is of military importance, the local geography, the risk of endemic dangers—such as flood and earthquake—and a host of rare calamities. There is no way to precisely assess the risk to the integrity of your infrastructure, but it's certainly non-zero.

I am fairly safe in California. I could hike a few days to reach the agricultural regions of the valley, or grow my own food given seeds, a field, and a summer season. What would happen to you?

Living in cities presents a tradeoff between risk and reward: more jobs but more crime, better health care but worse pollution. We make risk assessments every day when we use electricity, drive a car, or take a bath. Exposure to some danger is inevitable, but to increase your chance of survival, actively consider whether the risks you take are sensible. That's what's known as common sense!

The ultimate urban disaster novel:
Earth Abides by George R. Stewart

Do you live in a city? Prepare or despair! And while you're at it, despair over the plight of the criminals in the following stories who mastermind their own misfortune while engaged in their chosen trade.

DARWIN AWARD: HUMAN POPSICLE

2000 *Darwin Award Runner-Up*
Confirmed by Darwin
24 JANUARY 2000, OHIO

The Los Angeles Police Department contacted Ohio police hoping to locate a missing truck driver and his load of broccoli. The stalled truck was located in Ohio four days later and towed to a local mechanic. They thawed and refueled the truck and found that, apart from an empty gas tank, the vehicle had no mechanical problems, but the driver's personal effects and seven bricks of marijuana were discovered in the cab of the vehicle.

The trucking company and the police were both interested in the whereabouts of the errant driver, and a search was initiated. Shortly thereafter a patrolman noticed two feet protruding from between the pallets of broccoli—feet which belonged to the missing man.

The broccoli was unloaded as quickly as possible in the cold Ohio winter, leaving the frozen body of the driver standing precisely upside down, attached to the floor of the trailer by his head. He was surrounded by space heaters and eventually pried off the floor, but his frigid corpse, arm extended, had to be turned on its side to maneuver it into a rescue squad vehicle.

Police in Wichita, Kansas, arrested a twenty-two-year-old man at an airport hotel after he tried to pass two counterfeit $16 bills.

(Honorable Mention of unknown veracity, culled from a decade of email.)

The Cuyahoga County coroner's office determined that the man had been trying to retrieve a stash of cocaine from between the pallets of broccoli when he fell and knocked himself unconscious. He soon suffered a fatal case of hypothermia and died in the icy air. Perhaps this unfortunate soul should have confined his drug smuggling to the more clement climate of California.

Reference: Richfield Township, Ohio, Police Department Incident #00514
 ANOTHER TRAGIC THEFT: Wrong Time, Wrong Place, page 197

DARWIN AWARD: SKI THEFT BACKFIRES
Confirmed by Darwin
FEBRUARY 1998, CALIFORNIA

Darrell and his friends stole a foam pad from the legs of a Mammoth Mountain ski lift, piled onto it, and slid down a ski run at 3 A.M. on their makeshift sledge. The foam pad, lacking any steering or safety features, crashed into a lift tower which was—by amazing coincidence—the same tower from which it had been stolen. Lacking the cushion of foam meant to protect errant skiers, the tower was an obstacle too hard for Darrell to overcome. There's a moral in there somewhere . . .

Reference: *Guardian, Sacramento Bee*

🖉 ANOTHER SELF-CORRECTING THEFT: Junk Food Junkie, page 195

When two service station attendants in Ionia, Michigan, refused to hand over the cash to an intoxicated robber, the man threatened to call the cops. The attendants still wouldn't give him the money, so the robber called the police, waited for them to arrive—and was arrested.

(Honorable Mention of unknown veracity, culled from a decade of email.)

Darwin Award: Escaping Conviction

Confirmed by Darwin

December 1997, Pennsylvania

A prisoner in the new Allegheny County Jail in Pittsburgh attempted to evade his punishment by engineering an escape from his confinement. Jerome constructed a hundred-foot rope of bedsheets, broke through a supposedly shatter-proof cell window, and began to climb to freedom down his makeshift ladder.

It is not known whether his plan took into account the curiosity of drivers on the busy street and Liberty Bridge below. It certainly did not take into account the sharp edges of the glass, the worn nature of the bedsheet, or the great distance to the pavement. The bottom of the knotted bedsheet was eighty-six feet short of the ground. But our hero did not reach the end of his rope. The windowpane sliced through the weak cloth and dropped him to his untidy demise 150 feet below.

But wait, there's more!

Apparently the jailhouse rumor of the previous death did not reach a prisoner who was awaiting transfer to a federal penitentiary one year later. He tied eight bedsheets together and rappelled from his seventh-floor window, only to find that the rope fell twenty-five feet short of the ground. Luckier than Jerome, he merely fractured his ankle and scraped his face.

Reference: *Pittsburgh Post-Gazette*

Another fall from a great height: Lawnchair Larry, page 200

DARWIN AWARD: KILLING TIME

Unconfirmed by Darwin

2001, SCOTLAND

Electric trains in Glasgow collect power from the overhead cable and transmit any excess through the rails to a solid copper cable that routes it to a power redistribution box.

Copper is a favorite target for thieves. One enterprising fellow with a good knowledge of the electrical system planned to cut the copper cable during the time between trains, when no electricity was traveling through it. His plan might have worked . . . but for one small flaw.

In the pocket of his charred overcoat, police found an out-of-date rail timetable. The train arrived ten minutes before he thought it would, sending hundreds of volts of electricity through the thief's hacksaw and into his body, and putting an untimely end to his career.

MORE ENTERPRISING MEN LOOKING FOR A FREE RIDE:
Dodging Drink Dues, page 48

Is this electrocution death possible? Several residents of Glasgow wrote in to say they never heard of this train sizzler, and what's more, Glasgow trains are so unreliable that no one would trust his life to a timetable, accurate or not. Electrically minded readers reported that current flows through the overhead wires all the time, not just when trains pass. One theorized, "You'd have to be pretty clever to know enough about electricity and the underground system to consider pulling this one off. My guess is he heard someone discussing the idea in a pub and decided to give it a whirl whilst in a chemical haze." Myself I find it plausible because thieves regularly electrocute themselves while stealing copper. What are they doing, recycling?

More Reader Comments:

"This often happens in South Africa. Thieves go for the thick copper bus bars or the high voltage overhead lines so often the deaths don't even make the news. I have photos of bodies and limbs still attached to the cables."

"When the train picks up power, it needs a ground contact to complete the circuit. It grounds through the perfectly ordinary rails. However these rails are not designed to be electrically sound, so they back them up with a copper wire which connects to the rails at regular intervals. Normally this cable remains at zero voltage and is perfectly safe to steal. However when a train passes, a high current passes through it, and will flow through the thief and into the earth. It only takes 80 milliamps to kill."

DARWIN AWARD: JUST SAY NO!

Confirmed by Darwin

29 NOVEMBER 2000, CANADA

A police officer who regularly lectured addiction counselors on the dangers of illicit drugs proved that actions speak louder than words when he was found dead of a heroin overdose. He had taken heroin and cocaine from police exhibits "without filing the proper forms" and apparently overdosed while experimenting with the narcotics. He unfortunately didn't heed the creed written on his own patrol car: "Say no to drugs!"

Reference: *Toronto Globe and Mail*

AN OVERDOSE OF A DIFFERENT SORT: Liposuction Tragedy, page 14

A man wearing pantyhose on his head tried to rob a shopping mall store. When store security made an appearance, he quickly grabbed a market basket and pretended to be shopping—forgetting that he was still wearing the pantyhose. He was captured and his loot returned.

(Honorable Mention of unknown veracity, culled from a decade of email.)

DARWIN AWARD: STAB IN THE DARK

Unconfirmed by Darwin

3 DECEMBER 2000, AUSTRALIA

The death of a man in the suburbs of Brisbane was precipitated by a bizarre twist of fate. The twenty-one-year-old and his friend went to a trailer park intent on doing some serious damage to the occupant of one particular mobile home. In the ensuing confusion, the intended victim escaped without injury while his two attackers managed to viciously stab one another. The younger knife-wielder died at the scene, and his older friend was hospitalized with severe injuries. The incident thus qualifies for both a Darwin Award and an Honorable Mention, a rare event indeed!

Reference: Australian Broadcasting Corporation

FRIENDS DON'T LET FRIENDS INCITE MAYHEM: Throwing Stones, page 16

Police in Radnor, Pennsylvania, interrogated a suspect by placing a metal colander on his head and connecting wires from it to a photocopy machine. They placed the message "HE'S LYING" in the copier and pressed the copy button each time they thought the suspect wasn't telling the truth. Believing the lie detector was working, the suspect confessed to the police.

(Honorable Mention of unknown veracity, culled from a decade of email.)

DARWIN AWARD: YOU SAID A MOUTHFUL
Confirmed by Darwin
18 MAY 2001, ILLINOIS

A Chicago woman took revenge into her own hands quite successfully when she bit off the testicles of her rapist during the attack. The twenty-one-year-old man should have known better than to accost a woman twice his age and ferocity. When he dropped his trousers and forced her down, she seized her opportunity and severed his gonads, rendering him permanently sterile, to the satisfaction of all but the eunuch.

The woman walked to police headquarters a block away and turned the testicles over to police. Shortly thereafter a man with a matching injury appeared at the Michael Reese Medical Center. Police put two and two together and cordoned off the injured man's hospital room, while doctors attempted, unsuccessfully, to reattach the rapist's genitals.

A hospital spokesperson confirms that our Darwin Award winner is now sterile.

Reference: *Chicago Tribune*, Reuters
ANOTHER SATISFYING REVENGE: Call Girl, page 164
ANOTHER TOOTHSOME HUMAN MORSEL: Eat the Young, page 40

Honorable Mention: The Sting

Confirmed by Darwin

2001, California

"You won the lottery!"

California fugitives hoping to collect $1,500 in lottery winnings walked into a police sting aimed at serving outstanding felony warrants. The nonexistent Fresno County Lottery Commission sent thirty-two hundred letters, claiming to be distributing $78 million in excess lottery funds. The winners were instructed to present identification at the County Fairgrounds.

They arrived to find a balloon and streamer-festooned building, where they left their smiling relatives as one by one they were called into separate rooms to receive their surprise.

Uniformed officers were standing by to explain the hoax and arrest the befuddled fugitives. The operation served eighty-one felony warrants and seventy-five arrests, and a surveillance team arrested two men on suspicion of car burglary.

Reference: *Fresno Bee*, and Mom

Another example of captors more clever than their prey:
Bodacious Bud, page 165

HONORABLE MENTION: FERGUSON 2, THIEVES 0

Confirmed by Darwin
JANUARY 2001, ENGLAND

Two men were taken to a Liverpool hospital after trying to burgle the house of pro soccer player Duncan Ferguson. The soccer
player in question has earned the nicknames Duncan Disorderly
and Drunken Ferguson for his aggressive behavior on and off the
field. He once headbutted a policeman, and spent six months in
jail for injuring an opponent. This six-foot-four kamikaze center
forward is arguably the most violent player in British pro football, and not the best choice of victim. Police arrived quickly to
rescue the miscreants from Duncan's wrath. Only one of the
hapless burglars required hospitalization.

Reference: *Sentinal*, BBC Radio News, UK National Newspapers

ANOTHER UNSUCCESSFUL ATTEMPT TO RUN FROM MENACE:
A Fell Death, page 96

The weekly aviation newsletter *AVweb* reported that a burglar
broke into a Mooney aircraft at the Knox County, Ohio, airport
and removed its avionics system, including the Emergency Locating Transmitter. This device sends homing signals if the aircraft
crashes. During the getaway run, the ham-handed crook jarred
the ELT enough to activate it, and authorities had no trouble
tracking the perpetrator to his lair.

(Honorable Mention of unknown veracity, culled from a decade of email.)

HONORABLE MENTION: MORSEL OF EVIDENCE

Confirmed by Darwin

16 MAY 2001, NEW ZEALAND

Cruising police spotted a longtime member of the Mongrel Mob sitting in a parked car in Hastings. The officers stopped and searched his vehicle, unearthing a plastic baggie presumed to be full of drugs.

While the thug was being questioned about the contents of the bag, he suddenly grabbed the drugs and began to scuffle with police. He was subdued with pepper spray and a restraining hold, and police began to search for the missing baggie. Their captive, meanwhile, had become strangely subdued. He was white as a sheet and no longer breathing.

Turns out he had swallowed the plastic bag, which the officers discovered during their resuscitation efforts stuck far down his throat. They extracted the baggie with the help of pliers from a pocket Leatherman, and the man revived.

Saved from a Darwin Award despite himself, he was jailed on drug and assault charges along with thirteen other suspected gang members whose seized booty totaled $30,000 in drugs and stolen property.

Reference: *Dominion*

ANOTHER STORY ABOUT INGESTING DRUGS: Just Say No!, page 158

HONORABLE MENTION: CALL GIRL

Confirmed by Darwin

25 APRIL 2001, NEW YORK

"Why don't you come back and meet me here?" He thought she was calling to arrange a hot date, but he was wrong. The twenty-nine-year-old rapist had not only assaulted his victim, but also stolen $70 and her cell phone after poking her in the neck with a pair of tweezers he took from her purse.

As soon as he left her apartment, she summoned help, and police encouraged her to assist in the capture of the rapist. Under their watchful eye, she called him on her own cell phone and courageously coaxed him back to her building.

The woman was an excellent actress. Her attacker arrived for his "date" an hour later with a forty-ounce bottle of Heineken in his hand and her panties and cell phone tucked in his pocket. Police took the man, trailing a long criminal record, into custody.

His victim really did a number on him.

Reference: *New York Post*

ANOTHER MAN WHOSE MANHOOD IS IN QUESTION: Lobster Vasectomy, page 124

ANOTHER RINGING PHONE BRINGS TROUBLE: Midnight Special, page 196

HONORABLE MENTION: BODACIOUS BUD

Unconfirmed by Darwin

2000, INDIANA

A gardener had the good fortune to raise a healthy marijuana plant in his backyard. But then terror struck! He received a phone call from the authorities saying he was busted . . . but they would not press charges if he brought the bush into the station, roots and all.

So he sadly hacked down his eight-foot annual and carried it into the lobby of the sheriff's office, where startled officers took him into custody for suspected felony cultivation.

Turns out the phone call was a prank.

Reference: *Indiana Bedford Times-Mail*

MORE MARIJUANA: Human Popsicle, page 152

HONORABLE MENTION: SIPHON!

Unconfirmed by Darwin
2000, WASHINGTON

When a man attempted to siphon gasoline from a motor home parked on a residential Seattle street, he got much more than he had bargained for. Police arrived at the scene to find a violently ill thief curled up retching next to a motor home, surrounded by spilled sewage. A police spokesman said that once he recovered, the man admitted to trying to steal gasoline from the parked vehicle, but he plugged his hose into the motor home's sewage tank by mistake. The owner of the vehicle declined to press charges, saying that it was the best laugh he'd ever had.

ANOTHER SEWAGE STORY: **Sewer Shower,** page 54

A Los Angeles man who later said he was "tired of walking" stole a steamroller and led police on a five-mile-per-hour chase, until an officer stepped aboard and brought the vehicle to a halt. (Honorable Mention of unknown veracity, culled from a decade of email.)

Honorable Mention: Planning Ahead

Unconfirmed by Darwin

February 2000, England

Warning to crooks: Don't expect the victim to cooperate with your plans! A bank robber presented a note at a cashier's window, threatening to hack into their computer system unless they handed over a large sum of money. When he returned later that day to collect his cash, police were standing by to nab him.

Reference: *London Metro*

Another threat backfires: Moscow Marauder, page 20

A man walked into a Circle-K store in Louisiana, put a $20 bill on the counter, and asked for change. When the clerk opened the cash drawer, the man pulled a gun and asked for all the cash in the register, which the clerk promptly provided. The man took the cash and fled, leaving his $20 bill on the counter. The money he took from the drawer totaled $15. If someone points a gun at you and gives you money, is a crime committed?

(Honorable Mention of unknown veracity, culled from a decade of email.)

HONORABLE MENTION: SOBRIETY TEST
Unconfirmed by Darwin
15 MAY 2001

In a poorly judged attempt to convince his wife he was sober enough to drive, a twenty-nine-year-old man pulled up to a State Police barracks in his pickup truck, parked illegally, and demanded a sobriety check. He failed the Breathalyzer test and was taken into custody. "Basically," an amused Sergeant Paul Slevinski explained, "his wife won the argument."

Reference: *Southampton Press*

ANOTHER MAN WHO TURNED HIMSELF IN: Dumb Drunk, page 39

Darwin Awards: Keeping a Date with Dense-ity

Personal Account: Medical Misadventures

I have three stories to share, two published in a professional magazine and the third a personal account which is sadly unverifiable but absolutely true.

The first story is described in a lawsuit filed against a veterinarian and his clinic by the grieving family of a young man who had been hired three weeks previously and trained for kennel work: dog walking, animal feeding, poop scooping, etc. He was found dead by his supervisor midway through his first day of solo work. His body was lying in the surgery suite, a place a kennel worker has no business being, wrapped around an empty bottle of liquid anesthetic gas.

Apparently this Darwin wannabe had sought the drug out and chugged down the whole bottle in the hopes that it would give him a euphoric high. He did not realize that the liquid is vaporized into a gas before being administered to patients. In its highly concentrated liquid form, it probably killed him before he had the chance to realize he wasn't getting a buzz.

The kicker to this story is that his family is suing the veterinarian and the clinic for not providing their idiot child with appropriate training. What sort of training do you need in order to avoid, and especially not ingest, unknown substances? Did they have to tell him not to drink the bleach? "Hey, kid, don't mess with those scalpel blades, but if you do, be sure not to jam one up your nose."

The second story is from a series of articles about controlled drugs—those drugs with abuse potential—and how to keep your clinic's supply safe and legal. Ketamine, an injectible anesthetic known on the street as Special K, is a popular target for veterinary drug thieves. The clinic in the article had suffered a break-in and was missing several bottles of Ketamine and, oddly, two bottles of euthanasia solution as well.

Euthanasia solution is the highly concentrated form of an injectible anesthetic that is used to humanely end the lives of suffering animals. The product label makes it extremely clear that the purpose of the drug is to kill. A skull and crossbones is a prominent feature on the packaging.

The thieves were found a few days later, sprawled amid the cash from the sale of their stolen Ketamine. They didn't have a chance to enjoy their booty, however, as one was dead and the second comatose from injecting the concentrated euthanasia solution directly into their veins.

The third story involves a telephone call we received one Saturday while I was working at a veterinary emergency hospital. I heard my technician answer the phone, listen, and say, "Hold on, I'll ask the doctor." He turned to me and gave me a drug name that sounded familiar, but I couldn't place it, nor could I find it in my drug dictionary.

I asked him to interrogate the caller. Were they clients? Had we prescribed the drug? If not, where had they found it and why were they calling me instead of the hospital? Maybe with more information I could answer their question.

He went back to the phone and clarified the situation. He put the callers on hold and said, "They bought the drug on the street in Mexico and just shot it up. They want to know what it is supposed to do to them." Apparently the bottle was labeled in Spanish, and one recognizable word resembled the English word "veterinary." That was why they called me to ask why the drug wasn't giving them the promised high.

I wish I had had the foresight to pretend it was a concentrated hormone that causes testicular shrinkage, but instead I saved them from winning a Darwin Award by telling them to get their stupid selves to the nearest human emergency room.

Reference: *DVM Newsmagazine* and J. S. Vanderholm, personal account.
ANOTHER CALL FOR HELP: That Sinking Feeling, page 34

According to the FBI, most modern-day bank robberies are "unsophisticated and unprofessional crimes" committed by young male repeat offenders who apparently don't know the first thing about their trade. For instance it is reported that in spite of the widespread use of surveillance cameras, 76 percent of bank robbers wear no disguise, 86 percent never study the bank before robbing it, and 95 percent make no long-range plans for concealing the loot. Thus the FBI offers this advice to would-be bank robbers: Consider another line of work.

Top Twelve FBI Homicides
www.DarwinAwards.com/book/fbi.html

CHAPTER 9

Disqualified:
Losing Is Its Own Reward

You run and you run
to catch up with the sun
but it's sinking, and racing around
to come up behind you again.

The sun is the same in a relative way
but you're older,
shorter of breath,
and one day closer to death.

—Pink Floyd, *Dark Side of the Moon*

Some deaths deserve a Darwin and some don't. Nominees are occasionally disqualified by readers correcting my judgment or knowledge. The following stories are not Darwins. Here's why.

NOT A DARWIN: DO BIKES FLOAT?
JUNE 1999

A boy afraid he'd lose his bicycle lost a far more valuable possession instead—his life. The setting was the Atlantic Ocean, in a seaside town where the rambunctious youth and his family were vacationing. One day he decided to copy the local boys and ride his bicycle off the pier into the water. But he didn't want to lose his wheels to the surging waves!

So he tied the handlebar firmly to his wrist, and sped off the end of the pier. Unfortunately bicycles don't float. He was pulled under and drowned while frantic police and bystanders tried to help. Eventually the boy's body was recovered from fifteen feet of water.

The moral of the story? Don't do as the locals do.

Darwinian Rule Violation:
Victim not mature.

When this was nominated for a Darwin, members of the seaside town immediately began a letter campaign requesting that I remove the nomination. The boy was only copying what he'd seen on TV, they said. He was new in town, unfamiliar with the ocean, and didn't understand the danger of sinking. He was a well-loved kid and the community who had tried in vain to rescue him grieved for his absence. Besides, they pointed out, my own rules say "mature only need apply." *They convinced me that this was an accident born of youth and suggestibility, not willful stupidity, and the nomination was withdrawn.*

Not a Darwin: Underwire Bras Deadly
September 1999, London

Two women became victims of fashion when their underwire bras acted as electrical conductors. The ladies were enjoying a break from shopping by taking a walk in Hyde Park, when a thunderstorm drove them under a tree for shelter. The Thailand natives were struck by a bolt of lightning, which killed them instantly.

Their bodies were ignored by other walkers until the following day, when it became apparent that they were not simply sleeping vagrants.

Forensic evidence revealed that the lightning discharge was channeled into the metal brassieres, leaving burn marks on the women's chests. The coroner stated that it was only the second time in his experience of fifty thousand deaths where an underwire brassiere was implicated in a fatal electrocution. The inquest recorded a verdict of death by misadventure.

Darwinian Rule Violation:
Accident—not self-inflicted, and lacks veracity.

Not even close to a Darwin! Women wear underwire bras the world over, and these two women's charged encounter was a random electrocution, not the result of a terminally stupid decision. *Besides I suspect it's an urban legend, so no Darwin!*

NOT A DARWIN:
TEXAS A&M BONFIRE

The Texas Aggies took themselves too seriously recently. It began on Thanksgiving Eve in 1999. Twelve students were crushed
while constructing a tower of logs intended for the traditional
"Bonfire" during the big football rally. As with every tragic loss
of lives, the deceased students and the University were repeatedly nominated for Darwin Awards by enthusiastic aficionados.

Texas A&M Bonfire Flames: Great thesis project!
www.DarwinAwards.com/book/bonfire.html

Darwinian Rule Violation:
Accident—not self-inflicted.

The Texas Aggies rebelled at finding this travesty suggested on the Internet. I received thousands of emails from irate students and grieving survivors. Their flames were notable in quantity and vehemence, and in their peculiar usage of the word "Bonfire" as a proper noun. Some of the more pithy pronouncements: "If I could take what you know about the quality of a life and roll it into a little bitty ball and shove it up a gnat's butt it would rattle around like a BB in a Mason jar." "Whoever is in charge should shoot themselves in the heads." "Repent of your sins." One writer promised to scoop out my testicles with a rusty spoon, little realizing that I don't even have testicles!

I did not let their anger sway my judgment. Even though the clout of the Texas Aggies is legendary—Steve Bensen, for example, was temporarily drubbed out of the *Arizona Republic* newspaper over his Bonfire cartoon—I was determined to consider the nomination on its own merits.

Fortunately for my health, after reading the reports on the accident and auditing the exhaustive Philosophy Forum discussions, I disqualified the nomination. Though the boozing students were driving heavy machinery and working on the Bonfire after-hours, the men and women who were squashed were not responsible for the poor design that caused the structure to collapse. *They were innocent victims, and not eligible for a Darwin Award.*

NOT A DARWIN: BODY CANYONING
JULY 1999, SWITZERLAND

An unusual sport called "body canyoning" claimed the lives of nineteen people in Bern, with two more missing and presumed dead.

Practitioners of body canyoning don life jackets and leap into white-water rapids, swimming and climbing through narrow river gorges in a race to go the farthest the fastest. Outfitting companies in the Swiss Alps provide river guides for body canyoning excursions.

This excursion group had been warned by mountain guards to expect heavy rain in the next few hours. But the unfortunate daredevils were woefully underprepared for the weather. A flash flood swept through the Saxteen River canyon, burying them under mud and debris.

The victims were from Britain, Australia, New Zealand, South Africa, and Switzerland.

Darwinian Rule Violation:
Accident—not self-inflicted.

This oft-submitted nomination received high scores from enthusiastic readers. But it's not a Darwin! The responsible parties were the employees of the river guide company, not the tourists hoping to spend happy days in supervised river play. This is one of many nominations involving accidents suffered during outdoor sporting activities, such as skiers crushed by an overloaded gondola falling from the cable. *Random tragedies in scenic locations don't win Darwin Awards!*

NOT A DARWIN: OUR BRIGHTEST CHEERLEADERS
MAY 2000, OKLAHOMA

Memorial Day weekend is a perfect excuse to drive to the lake and have some fun. Three cheerleaders stopped at a gas station to inflate their air mattresses, then continued happily on their way to the lake, unaware that they had filled the inflatables with oxyacetylene gas instead of air.

One of the cheerleaders lit a cigarette, and the rest is history.

A cheerleading coach described the three sixteen-year-olds as the best and brightest kids in the school. The girls recovered from severe burns in intensive care.

Darwinian Rule Violation:
No death, and an accident—not self-inflicted.

Disqualified July 2000 because the girls weren't responsible for mistaking the oxyacetylene gas nozzle for an air hose. Would you notice what was presumably an employee's mistake when filling *your* pool inflatables? Oxyacetylene is one of the most flammable gas mixtures available. It burns hotter than acetylene because the gas is accompanied by its own oxygen supply. Smoking around this gas is expressly verboten, as these girls learned to their dismay. *But they don't win a Darwin because they weren't lacking common sense. They were unfortunate victims of rotten luck.*

NOT A DARWIN: FATAL CASE OF HICCUPS
30 JUNE 2000, MARYLAND

A Baltimore man died after asking a friend to punch him in the chest to cure his hiccups. He had complained of hiccups after drinking several beers, and proposed this unusual remedy to his companion. The friend complied with his request, though with a distinct lack of enthusiasm, and the hiccup victim slumped to the ground outside a pizza shop. Friends summoned paramedics, but it was too late. The man had perished from his own terminally effective hiccup cure. No charges were filed against the puncher, who was merely following orders.

Darwinian Rule Violation:
Event lacks excellence.

Hiccups are an automatic reflex and an extended bout can be very painful. There are dozens of popular relief measures, including drinking water upside-down or swallowing thrice with a plugged nose. It turns out that approximately 1/100 of the heartbeat cycle is spent in a peculiarly sensitive state, and a short sharp shock at that precise instant can disrupt the heart and send a person into fatal cardiac fibrillation. But who knew it was so dangerous? *I might have done the same thing. It's not a Darwin.*

NOT A DARWIN: ICE FLOE FROLIC
MARCH 2001, NEWFOUNDLAND

When high winds blow ice floes into sheltered coastal harbors, residents enjoy leaping from floe to floe in a sport called "copying." The game is typically played on calm water close to shore. If you slip, as one tends to do on slick ice, you get wet feet and nothing more. But four teenagers decided to try their hand on the choppy waters of an unsheltered cove fifty meters from shore.

The young men were capering about on the ice floes, jumping from one to another, when one lost his footing and fell into the freezing water. He slid under the "slob ice," a treacherous sea of table-sized chunks, and disappeared. His three friends tried to rescue him, but in doing so forgot the adage about never turning your back on the ocean. Two were knocked into the icy soup and also drowned. One lucky teenager, sadly unable to save his friends, managed to reach shore.

A resident stated that the teens were very good boys who knew the danger of ice-jumping. "Hopefully the children in this area will learn a lesson from this."

Darwinian Rule Violation:
Accident—not self-inflicted.

Disqualified 21 May 2001 based on numerous complaints from residents of the cove declaring that the facts were incorrect. The letters culminated in an email from the news editor of the reporting newspaper: "Your Darwin Awards nomination concerning four Pouch Cove boys who were allegedly copying when they drowned is inaccurate. Early reports suggested they were copying, but in fact one fell in the water from shore and two more drowned trying to save him." *Based on the emails and the newspaper editor's explicit repudiation, I've removed it from consideration as a Darwin.*

NOT A DARWIN: SHOTGUN PEPSI
JULY 1999, NEW HAMPSHIRE

A ten-year-old boy experimenting with a weird way of drinking Pepsi pushed a plastic pushpin into his can, and began to suck on the hole. He may have been trying to "shotgun" the Pepsi by squirting it out of a small opening directly into his mouth. Unfortunately the pressurized tack shot from the can and lodged in his windpipe. Officers and neighbors attempted CPR without success.

Carbon dioxide bubbles had claimed another victim.

Neighbors mourned the child. "They all loved that little guy, as a matter of fact," said one. "He was a sweet, good-natured child from a family that holds hands. This is the all-American family." His fourth-grade teacher said, "This is the darkest hour of my teaching." Three siblings and his parents, both schoolteachers, survive.

Darwinian Rule Violation:
Victim not mature.

Readers loved and loathed this nominee: "I feel bad submitting this, but it's a truly moronic way to die." "Apparently pop-top technology is challenging our species' intelligence." "Every parent's nightmare." "The young man's untimely demise was either now or eight years down the road, as a fraternity pledge." "People should warn their children of the dire consequences." "Unbelievably tragic." "The child was too young to win!"

In the end I decided to remove the nomination from the website, because I believed that the lad was just experimenting with pushpins and Pepsi. That's what kids do—experiment with stuff. Who gave him the tacks anyway? *It was not a truly foreseeable demise, but rather a sad and freakish accent. No Darwin for this one!*

NOT A DARWIN: MANIA STRIKES BACK
AUGUST 1999, GERMANY

Police made a gruesome discovery when they found the emaciated and partly decomposed body of a seventy-five-year-old woman in her apartment. She had been dead for several weeks. Police said the old woman was a victim of her own collecting mania.

The rooms of her apartment were full of appliances, food, clothing, and filed brochures. A stack of items in the hall had collapsed and partly buried the woman. Unable to free herself, she died of thirst.

She lived alone in her flat and rarely contacted neighbors, so her death was not immediately noticed. Eventually, residents called the police to report a foul stench emanating from the apartment.

The police found fifty tins of fish, piles of toothpaste tubes, thirty flashlights, ten big leather suitcases, and rows of neatly filed advertisements. Only a few square meters of hallway were still inhabitable.

Darwinian Rule Violation:
Victim incapable of sound judgment.

Not a Darwin! Police refer to this behavior as Compulsive Collector Syndrome and consider it a mental illness. The story was disqualified as a Darwin Award nominee in September 2000. One reader presented a particularly compelling position against the nomination:

"Thanks for the enjoyment from this rare pile of humor. However I have reservations about Mania Strikes Back. The old lady was suffering from mental illness and not responsible for what happened. Illness should not be confused with stupidity. The cause may not be genetic; it may stem from emotional distress brought on by loneliness and isolation. Odd behavior and even suicide are a common result. This story belongs in a section called. 'Old women that would not go crazy if they had some money to make their children come visit them in their stinking rat homes.' *Mental illness is a disease like Parkinson's or Alzheimer's, and outside the scope of the Darwins.*"

Perhaps you wonder how police locate long-dead corpses such as this old woman's, or bodies in woods and hills. They train search dogs on scents like these from Sigma-Aldrich:

- Sigma Pseudo™ Corpse Scent Formulation I.
  For early detection or below 0°C.
- Sigma Pseudo™ Corpse Scent Formulation II.
  For post-putrification detection.
- Sigma Pseudo™ Corpse Scent Drowned Victim Formulation. Valuable training aid for water search. Provides a reliable scent source for 30 to 45 minutes in still or running water.
- Sigma Pseudo™ Distressed Body Scent Trauma and Fear formulation for the detection of live victims of natural disaster or violent crime.

CHAPTER 10

Classic Dozen:
Better Read than Dead

Age cannot wither her,
nor custom stale her infinite variety.

—William Shakespeare, *Antony and Cleopatra*

These traditional commemorations of vast stupidity are a must-have in every mental collection. Enjoy re-reading your favorites: the twelve cream of the crop from the twentieth century.

Discussion: Speciation

One of the central questions of biology is how new species emerge.

New species grow from the roots of existing stock. Every species contains members with a variety of traits that originate from random mutations. Divide the population into two groups that don't interbreed, put the groups in different environments with different selective pressures, and they will begin to diverge as traits that are more (or less) favored increase (or dwindle) over time. Toss in a continual supply of random mutations, and you have the recipe for creating two species from one.

The process of speciation is similar to the manner by which new languages emerge, though it happens far more gradually. Recent speciations include the donkey and the horse, which can still crossbreed but produce sterile mule offspring, and the lion and the tiger, which produce sterile liger offspring.

There are many well-known examples of genetic variation caused by random mutations. Nectarines result from a hairless mutation of the peach, and vice-versa: each fruit orchard produces an occasional mutant sapling of the other fruit. The melanin content of human skin differs so that low levels of ambient sunlight can be used to manufacture enough Vitamin D in northern latitudes, while in sunny climes high levels of sunlight are blocked to protect against ultraviolet damage. Species possess an ever-changing palette of traits upon which selective pressures operate.

Species become divided into non-breeding groups by several means.

The most common division is geographical isolation, which may be caused by events as vast as continental drift or as small as a group that travels into new territory and cannot find its way back. A murder of crows might be driven offshore by a violent storm and marooned on a distant land. The Galapagos Islands, where Charles Darwin made his pivotal observations, were home to a number of animals that had been separated from their kind and subsequently evolved into a new species. Many a science fiction novel follows a group of humans who colonize another planet, lose the means to return, and become something other than human.

Another possibility is that a species might find itself in a habitat with two ecological niches that offer incompatible survival strategies. Species can split to take advantage of each niche. For example, the owl and the hawk evolved from a common (but not immediate) ancestor to take advantage of nocturnal and diurnal survival strategies, as did the cricket and the grasshopper.

A number of other population bottlenecks eliminate interbreeding. Researchers have discovered separate species that can be crossed to produce fertile offspring with the help of technology, but have mating strategies so contrary that they never procreate in the wild. For instance, an insect might suffer a random mutation that causes it to respond to pheromones carried only by members of its own family, forever separating it

from other members of its species. Chronological change also isolates groups: over millennia a species evolves *away from itself* and can no longer interbreed, though it is difficult to test precisely when this occurs in the absence of a time-travel machine.

A million times and more separated populations have drifted apart, accumulated genetic differences, and gradually created the biodiversity that surrounds us today. Genetically isolated groups evolve apart on a non-converging path and form new species. Estranged brethren become true strangers as evolution separates man from beast, mammal from reptile, animal from plant.

> Biological oddities called "ring species" exist: a species that shades into a number of subspecies as it circles a region. The subspecies at the distant ends of the ring are distinct species and do not interbreed, though there exists a continuous set of intermediate forms. Classic examples are the herring gull and the lesser black-backed gulls *Larus argentatus* and *fuscus*, and the blotched and non-blotched California salamander *Ensatina eschscholtzii*.

And with that, I must conclude this chapter discussion without, Dear Reader, a convincing segue to the stories that follow. I came up with the following but discarded it in horror: "Just as a discussion of evolution is not complete without the classic mechanics of speciation, so is a book of Darwin Awards incomplete without the classic Darwin winners."

DARWIN AWARD: JATO

1995 Darwin Award Winner
Debunked by Darwin

The Arizona Highway Patrol were mystified when they came upon a pile of smoldering wreckage embedded in the side of a cliff rising above the road at the apex of a curve. The metal debris resembled the site of an airplane crash, but it turned out to be the vaporized remains of an automobile. The make of the vehicle was unidentifiable at the scene.

The folks in the lab finally figured out what it was, and pieced together the events that led up to its demise.

It seems that a former air force sergeant had somehow got hold of a Jet-Assisted Take-Off (JATO) unit. JATO units are solid-fuel rockets used to give heavy military transport airplanes an extra push for takeoff from short airfields.

Dried desert lakebeds are the location of choice for breaking the world ground vehicle speed record. The sergeant took the JATO unit into the Arizona desert and found a long, straight stretch of road. He attached the JATO unit to his car, jumped in, accelerated to a high speed, and fired off the rocket.

The facts, as best as could be determined, are as follows:

The operator was driving a 1967 Chevy Impala. He ignited the JATO unit approximately 3.9 miles from the crash site. This was established by the location of a prominently scorched and melted strip of asphalt. The vehicle quickly reached a speed of between 250 and 300 miles per hour and continued at that speed, under full power, for an additional twenty to twenty-five

seconds. The soon-to-be pilot experienced G-forces usually reserved for dogfighting F-14 jocks under full afterburners.

The Chevy remained on the straight highway for approximately 2.6 miles (fifteen to twenty seconds) before the driver applied the brakes, completely melting them, blowing the tires, and leaving thick rubber marks on the road surface. The vehicle then became airborne for an additional 1.3 miles, impacted the cliff face at a height of 125 feet, and left a blackened crater three feet deep in the rock.

Most of the driver's remains were not recovered; however, small fragments of bone, teeth, and hair were extracted from the crater, and fingernail and bone shards were removed from a piece of debris believed to be a portion of the steering wheel.

Ironically, a still-legible bumper sticker was found: "How do you like my driving? Dial 1-800-EAT-SHIT."

This Darwin Award is the most popular of all time. Considered true for years, it was later confirmed as an Urban Legend by the Arizona Department of Public Safety. The story fooled the judges in 1995, so JATO has been grandfathered in as the 1995 Darwin Award Winner.

ANOTHER MONUMENTAL EXPLOSION: Kaboom!, page 135

Officer Bob Stein of the Arizona Department of Public Safety talks about the JATO story. "I receive inquiries about accidents, drug busts, and investigations. About two years ago I picked up the phone and researched what has now become an Arizona myth. Even now I receive about five calls a month from people wanting to know, did it really happen?"

Read the Official Arizona JATO denial.
www.DarwinAwards.com/book/jato.html

DARWIN AWARD: JUNK FOOD JUNKIE

1994 Darwin Award Winner
Unconfirmed by Darwin

The 1994 Darwin Award went to the fellow who was killed by a Coke machine which toppled over on top of him as he was attempting to tip a free soda out of it.

Reference: Reuters, Morgunbladid of Iceland, *Kenya Times*

 MORE DANGEROUS DRINK CONSUMPTION: Ethanol Schmethanol, page 21

**Terminal stupidity is
a self-limiting disease.**

DARWIN AWARD: MIDNIGHT SPECIAL
1992 Darwin Award Winner
Unconfirmed by Darwin
21 DECEMBER 1992, NORTH CAROLINA

Jacob, forty-seven, accidentally shot himself to death in December in Newton when, awakening to the sound of a ringing telephone beside his bed, he reached for the phone but grabbed instead his loaded Smith & Wesson .38 Special, which discharged when he drew it to his ear.

Reference: *Hickory Daily Record*
MORE BAD AIM: Shell Shot, page 133

Ready, Fire, Aim!

DARWIN AWARD: WRONG TIME, WRONG PLACE

Unconfirmed by Darwin

3 FEBRUARY 1990, WASHINGTON

A man tried to commit a robbery in Renton, Washington. It was probably his first attempt at armed robbery, as suggested by the fact that he had no previous record of violent crime, and by his terminally stupid choices:

1. The target was H & J Leather and Firearms. A gun shop.
2. The shop was full of customers—firearms customers.
3. To enter the shop, the robber had to step around a marked police patrol car parked at the front door.
4. An officer in uniform was standing next to the counter, having coffee before reporting to duty.

Upon seeing the officer, the would-be robber announced a holdup and fired a few wild shots. The officer and a clerk promptly returned fire, covered by several customers who also drew their guns, thereby removing the confused criminal from the gene pool. No one else was hurt..

🐒 ANOTHER POORLY PLANNED HEIST: Planning Ahead, page 167

DARWIN AWARD: COUNT YOUR CHICKENS

1996 Darwin Award Winner
Confirmed by Darwin
31 AUGUST 1995, EGYPT

Six people drowned while trying to rescue a chicken that had fallen into a well in southern Egypt. An eighteen-year-old farmer was the first to descend into the sixty-foot well. He drowned, apparently after an undercurrent in the water pulled him down. Police said his sister and two brothers, none of whom could swim well, went down the well one by one to help him, but also drowned. Two elderly farmers then came by to help. But they were apparently pulled under by the same undercurrent. The bodies of the six were eventually extricated from the well in the village of Nazlat Imara, 240 miles south of Cairo.

The chicken was also pulled out. It survived.

Reference: Associated Press

ANOTHER STORY WITH MULTIPLE WINNERS:
Intersecting Darwins, page 67

Darwin Awards: Die and Learn

DARWIN AWARD: THE LAST SUPPER

1993 Darwin Award Winner
Unconfirmed by Darwin
25 MARCH 1993

A terrible diet and a room with no ventilation were blamed for the death of a man killed by his own gas. There were no marks found on his body, but an autopsy revealed the presence of large amounts of methane dissolved in his blood.

His diet had consisted primarily of beans and cabbage, just the right combination of foods to produce a severe gas attack. It appeared that the man died in his sleep from breathing the poisonous cloud that was hanging over his bed.

Had his windows been open, the flatulence wouldn't have been fatal, but they were sealed shut to create a nearly airtight bedroom. He was an obese man with an unlimited capacity for creating methane gas, and a deadly disregard for proper ventilation.

ANOTHER DEADLY ELIMINATION OF HUMAN WASTE:
Ur-inate-iot, page 94

Serious Flatulence Research:
www.DarwinAwards.com/book/farts.html

HONORABLE MENTION: LAWNCHAIR LARRY

Confirmed by Darwin

2 JULY 1982, CALIFORNIA

Larry Walters of Los Angeles is one of the few to contend for a Darwin Award and live to tell the tale. "I have fulfilled my twenty-year dream," said Walters, a former truck driver for a company that makes TV commercials. "I'm staying on the ground. I've proved the thing works."

Larry's boyhood dream was to fly. But fates conspired to keep him from his dream. He joined the air force, but his poor eyesight disqualified him from pilot status. After he was discharged from the armed services, he sat in his backyard watching jets fly overhead.

He hatched his weather-balloon scheme while sitting outdoors in his "extremely comfortable" Sears lawnchair. He purchased forty-five weather balloons from an Army-Navy surplus store, tied them to his tethered lawnchair—dubbed the *Inspiration I*—and filled the four-foot-diameter balloons with helium. Then he strapped himself into his lawnchair with some sandwiches, Miller Lite beer, and a pellet gun.

Larry's plan was to sever the anchor and lazily float up to a height of about thirty feet above his backyard, where he would enjoy a few hours of flight before coming back down. He figured he would pop a few brews, then pop a few of the forty-five balloons when it was time to descend, and gradually lose altitude. But things didn't work out quite as Larry planned.

When his friends cut the cord anchoring the lawnchair to his Jeep, he did not float lazily up to thirty feet. Instead, he streaked into the LA sky as if shot from a cannon, pulled by a lift of forty-five helium balloons holding thirty-three cubic feet of helium each. He didn't level off at a hundred feet, nor did he level off at a thousand feet. After climbing and climbing, he leveled off at sixteen thousand feet.

At that height he felt he couldn't risk shooting any of the balloons, lest he unbalance the load and really find himself in trouble. So he stayed there, drifting with his beer and sandwiches for several hours while he considered his options. At one point he crossed the primary approach corridor of Los Angeles' LAX airspace, and Delta and Trans-World airline pilots radioed in incredulous reports of the strange sight.

Eventually he gathered the nerve to shoot a few balloons, and slowly descended through the night sky. The hanging tethers tangled and caught in a power line, blacking out a Long Beach neighborhood for twenty minutes. Larry climbed to safety, where he was arrested by waiting members of the Los Angeles Police Department. As he was led away in handcuffs, a reporter dispatched to cover the daring rescue asked him why he had done it. Larry replied nonchalantly, "A man can't just sit around."

Reference: Associated Press, *Los Angeles Times, New York Times,* UPI, Crest REACT (a C.B. radio club), STABBED WITH A WEDGE OF CHEESE by Charles Downey, ALL I REALLY NEED TO KNOW I LEARNED IN KINDERGARTEN by Robert Fulghum

ANOTHER MAN WITH AN UNLIKELY PASSION: Grenade Juggler, page 131

Photographs of Lawnchair Larry
www.DarwinAwards.com/book/larry.html

Larry's efforts won him a $1,500 FAA fine, a prize from the Bonehead Club of Dallas, Texas, the altitude record for manned gas-filled clustered balloon flight, and a Darwin Awards Honorable Mention. He gave his aluminum lawnchair to admiring neighborhood children, abandoned his truck-driving job, and went on the lecture circuit, where he enjoyed intemittent demand as a motivational speaker. He never made much money from his innovative flight, never married, and had no children. Larry hiked into the forest and shot himself on October 6, 1993, at the age of forty-four.

**Forget the adage about learning
from your own mistakes.
It's safer and more entertaining
to learn from the mistakes of others!**

Honorable Mention: Revenge of the Gopher
Confirmed by Darwin
3 April 1995, California

Anyone who has watched the movie *Caddyshack* will have a good idea of the resilience of gophers. In the spring of 1995 three employees of the Carroll Fowler Elementary School in Ceres received a gopher in good condition. Their subsequent actions show that they were unfamiliar with the movie in particular, and with the vengeful nature of gophers in general.

One janitor and two maintenance men hauled the gopher into a small janitorial closet and apparently decided to kill it. There is no other plausible reason for spraying cleaning solvent on a gopher.

The solvent was designed to remove gum by freezing it and making it easier to scrape up. Elementary schools have an ongoing need for such solvents. But the gopher was stronger than the gum. Three cans later, it was still alive and kicking.

The men paused for a moment of silent reflection, and the janitor lit a cigarette in the fume-filled room. The subsequent explosion injured all three men, and sixteen children were treated for scraped knees.

In the aftermath, the persecuted gopher was discovered unharmed, clinging to a wall. He was released back into the wild, where he will enjoy years of free drinks in gopher pubs as he tells the story of his brush with death.

Reference: *Sacramento Bee, Hartford Courant*

Another explosion: Man with Gas Can, page 143

URBAN LEGEND: FROG GIGGIN' ACCIDENT
25 JULY 1996, ARKANSAS

Two local men were seriously injured when their pickup truck left the road and struck a tree near Cotton Patch on State Highway 38 early Friday morning. Woodruff County Deputy Dovey Snyder reported the accident shortly after midnight.

Thurston Poole, of Des Arc, and Billy Ray Wallis, of Little Rock, are listed in serious condition at Baptist Medical Center. The accident occurred as the two thirty-something men were returning to Des Arc after a frog giggin' excursion.

On an overcast Sunday night Poole's pickup truck headlights malfunctioned. The two men concluded that the headlight fuse on the older model truck had burned out. A replacement fuse was not available, but Wallis noticed that the twenty-two-caliber bullet from his pistol fit perfectly into the fuse box next to the steering wheel column. Upon insertion of the bullet, the headlights again began to operate properly and the two men proceeded eastbound toward the White River Bridge.

After they had traveled approximately twenty miles, just before crossing the river, the bullet apparently overheated, discharged, and struck Poole in the right testicle. The vehicle swerved sharply to the right, exiting the pavement and striking a tree. Poole suffered only minor cuts and abrasions from the accident but required surgery to repair the bullet wound. Wallis sustained a broken clavicle and was treated and released.

"Thank God we weren't on that bridge when Thurston [shot his intimate parts off] or we might have been dead," stated Wallis.

Upon being notified of the wreck, Poole's wife asked how many frogs the boys had caught.

ANOTHER STORY OF INGENUITY GONE WRONG: Ski Theft Backfires, page 154

Urban Legend:
Metallica Concert Misadventure
1996, Washington

Police in George, Washington, issued a report on the events leading up to the deaths of Robert Uhlenake, twenty-four, and his friend Ormond D. Young, twenty-seven, at a Friday night Metallica concert.

Uhlenake and Young were found dead at the Gorge Amphitheater soon after the show. Uhlenake was in a pickup that was on top of Young at the bottom of a twenty-foot drop. Young was found with severe lacerations, numerous fractures, contusions, and a branch in his anal cavity. He also had been stabbed, and his pants were in a tree above him some fifteen feet off the ground, adding to the mystery of the heretofore unexplained scene.

According to Commissioner-in-Charge Inoye Appleton, Uhlenake and Young had tried to get tickets for the sold-out concert. When they were unable to obtain tickets, the two decided to stay in the parking lot and drink. Once the show began, and after the two had consumed eighteen beers between them, they hit upon the idea of scaling the seven-foot wooden security fence around the perimeter of the site and sneaking in.

They moved the truck up to the edge of the fence and decided that Young would go over first and then assist Uhlenake. They did not count on the fact that, while it was a seven-foot fence on the parking lot side, there was a twenty-three-foot drop on the other side.

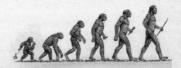

Young, who weighed 255 pounds and was quite inebriated, jumped up and over the fence and promptly fell about half the distance before a large tree branch broke his fall and his left forearm. He also managed to get his shorts caught on the branch. Since he was now in great pain and had no way to extricate himself and his shorts from the tree, he decided to cut his shorts off and fall to the bushes below.

As soon as he cut the last bit of fabric holding him on the branch, he suddenly plummeted the rest of the way down, losing his grip on the knife. The bushes he had depended on to break his fall were actually holly bushes, and landing in them caused a massive number of small cuts. He also had the misfortune to land squarely on a holly bush branch, effectively impaling himself. The knife, which he had accidentally released fifteen feet up, now landed and stabbed him in his left thigh. He was in tremendous pain.

Enter his friend Robert Uhlenake.

Uhlenake had observed the series of tumbles and realized that Young was in trouble. He hit upon the idea of lowering a rope to his friend and pulling him up and over the fence. This was complicated by the fact that Young outweighed Uhlenake by a good hundred pounds. Happily, despite his drunken state, Uhlenake realized he could use their truck to pull Young out. Unhappily, because of his drunken state, Uhlenake put the truck in reverse gear. He broke through the fence and landed on Young, killing him. Uhlenake was thrown from the truck and subsequently died of internal injuries.

"So that's how a dead 255-pound man with no pants on, with a truck on top of him and a stick up his ass, came to be," said Commissioner Appleton.

More inebriated behavior: Medical Misadventures, page 169

Urban Legend Status conferred December 31, 1997. Intensive searching of online Washington State newspapers failed to produce validation. The statement attributed to the commissioner is obviously bogus, as police do not make light of deadly shenanigans and never use the word *ass* to describe the rectum. And the Washington State sheriff's office disclaimed knowledge of this story.

Darwin Awards: Where Evolution Hits the Pavement

URBAN LEGEND:
SCUBA DIVERS AND FOREST FIRES
1998, CALIFORNIA

So you think you're having a bad day?

In California, wildfires are part of the natural cycle of the forest. They are caused by lightning, by arson, by acts of God. Brave firefighters earn their livings extinguishing these ravenous blazes.

Not long ago, fire marshals found a corpse in a rural section of California while they were assessing the damage done by a recent forest fire. The deceased male was dressed in diving gear consisting of a recently melted wet suit, a dive tank, flippers, and face mask. Apparently the man had been participating in recreational diving fairly recently.

A postmortem examination attributed his death not to burns, but to massive internal injuries. Salt water was found in his stomach. Dental records provided a positive identification of a man who had been reported missing a week before, and the next of kin were notified. Investigators then set about determining how a fully clad diver ended up in the middle of a forest fire.

It was discovered that, on the day of the fire, the deceased had set out on a diving trip in the Pacific Ocean. His third dive was twenty kilometers away from the location of a large brush fire, which was threatening the safety of a nearby town.

Firefighters, seeking to control the conflagration as quickly as possible, had called in a fleet of helicopters to saturate the area with water. The helicopters towed large buckets, which were dropped into the ocean for rapid filling, then flown to the fire and emptied.

You guessed it! One minute our diver was marveling at the fish species of the Pacific and in the next breath he found himself in a fire bucket three hundred meters in the air. He experienced rapid decompression caused by the altitude change, suddenly followed by a plummet into burning trees.

As a consolation to bereaved relatives, investigators calculated that the man extinguished 1.78 square meters of the fire, approximately the area covered by a splattered human body. Bereaved were also consoled by the knowledge that he had enjoyed two rewarding dives preceding his fatal third immersion.

Divers and pilots alike are being warned to remain on the alert. Divers are encouraged to remain calm if scooped from the water, and to hang on to the bucket when the water is dumped on the fire. Decompression chambers will be made available immediately upon landing.

ANOTHER OCEANIC ENCOUNTER: Feeding the Dolphins, page 122

URBAN LEGEND: DOG AND JEEP

A classic Urban Legend, one of the most popular of all time:

A fellow from Michigan buys himself a brand-new $30,000 Jeep Grand Cherokee for Christmas. He goes down to his favorite bar and celebrates his purchase by tossing down a few too many brews with his buddies. In one of those male-bonding rituals five of them decide to take his new vehicle for a test drive on a duck hunting expedition. They load up the Jeep with the dog, the guns, the decoys, and the beer, and head out to a nearby lake.

It's the dead of winter, and of course the lake is frozen, so they need to make a hole in the ice to create a natural landing area for the ducks and decoys. It is common practice in Michigan to drive your vehicle out onto the frozen lake, and it is also common (if slightly illegal) to make a hole in the ice using dynamite. Our fellows have nothing to worry about on that score, because one member of the party works for a construction team, and happened to bring some dynamite along. The stick has a short twenty-second fuse.

The group is all set up and ready for action. Their shotguns are loaded with duck pellets, and they have beer, warm clothes, and a hunting dog. Still chugging down a seemingly bottomless supply of six-packs, the group considers how to safely dynamite a hole through the ice. One of these rocket scientists points out that the dynamite should explode at a location far from where they are standing. Another notes the risk of slipping on the ice when running away from a burning fuse. So they eventually settle on a plan to light the fuse and throw the dynamite out onto the ice as far as possible.

There is a bit of contention over who has the best throwing arm, and eventually the owner of the Jeep wins that honor. Once that question is settled, he walks about twenty feet out and holds the stick of dynamite at the ready while one of his companions lights the fuse with a Zippo. As soon as he hears the fuse sizzle, he hurls it across the ice at a great velocity and runs in the other direction.

Unfortunately, a member of another species has spotted his master's arm motions and comes to an instinctive decision. Remember a couple of paragraphs back when I mentioned the vehicle, the beer, the guns, and the dog? Yes, the dog: a trained black Labrador, born and bred for retrieving, especially things thrown by his owner. As soon as dynamite leaves hand, the dog sprints across the ice, hell-bent on wrapping his jaws around that enticing stick-shaped object.

Five frantic fellows immediately begin hollering at the dog, trying to get him to stop chasing the dynamite. Their cries fall on deaf ears. Before you know it, the retriever is headed back to his owner, proudly carrying the stick of dynamite with the burning twenty-second fuse. The group continues to yell and wave their arms while the happy dog trots toward them. In a desperate act its master grabs his shotgun and fires at his own dog.

The gun is loaded with duck shot, and confuses the dog more than it hurts him. Bewildered, he continues toward his master, who shoots at man's best friend again. Finally comprehending that his owner has become insane, the dog runs for cover with his tail between his legs. And the nearest cover is right under the brand-new Jeep Grand Cherokee.

Boom! The dog and the Jeep are blown to bits and sink to the bottom of the lake, leaving a large ice hole in their wake. The stranded men stand staring at the water with stupid looks on their faces, and the owner of the Jeep is left to explain the misadventure to his insurance company.

Needless to say, they determined that sinking a vehicle in a lake by the illegal use of explosives is not covered under their policy, and the owner is still making $400 monthly payments on his brand-new Jeep at the bottom of the lake.

MORE PROOF THAT MEN IN GROUPS HAVE LOWER INTELLIGENCE: House Hunting Gone Awry, page 75

Just because you can doesn't mean you should.

Appendices

1. Website Biography

The Darwin Awards archive began on a Stanford University webserver in 1994. Its cynical view of the human species made it a favorite speaker in classrooms and campus pubs around the world. News of the website spread by word of mouth, and nominations culled by avid followers flew in from far and wide. As the number of stories in the archive grew, so did its acclaim.

Eventually the Darwin Awards became the most popular of Stanford's biomedical research websites. It was encouraged to matriculate to its own webserver, and DarwinAwards.com was born.

The website is the locus for official Darwin Awards and associated tales of misadventure. Nominees are submitted daily to a public Slush Pile. Visitors can vote on stories, win Darwiniana, and share their opinions on the Philosophy Forum—a community of free thinkers who debate the merits of controversial nominees and enjoy philosophical, political, and scientific conversations.

In April 2000 Webmaster Wendy and volunteer translators propelled the Darwin Awards into the ranks of the top 3,000 most-visited websites. DarwinAwards.com won dozens of awards and began to indulge in cigars and fruity umbrella drinks. Briefly profitable during two halcyon years of the Internet bubble, the website now languishes in genteel poverty in an uncharted backwater of the galaxy.

Stories in this book may include a URL directing you to a webpage with more information. All of the hyperlinks can be explored starting from this portal:

www.DarwinAwards.com/book

2. Author Biography

Wendy Northcutt studied molecular biology at UC Berkeley, then worked in a neuroscience research lab at Stanford University. She launched the Darwin Awards archive on a Stanford website, and emailed stories to a small list of friends.

When academia began to pall <-: she joined a start-up biotech company hoping to develop cancer and diabetes therapeutics, and continued to work on the Darwin Awards.

Eventually the lure of the Internet proved too strong to resist, and Wendy abdicated her laboratory responsibilities to pursue a more colorful career. She now works as a freelance webmaster and public speaker, and hones her skills on the Darwin Awards website, expanding the nominations, voting, and debate.

Wendy first learned of the concept of the Darwin Awards from her cousin Ian, a mildly eccentric philosopher who later started his own religion in order to avoid shaving his beard while working in the pizza industry. Ian is now pursuing a degree in archeology, and his hair is not an issue.

Wendy devotes her free time to studying human behavior, writing Darwin Awards, and forming eccentric opinions while reading, traveling, and gardening.

3. Forum Decorum

The Philosophy Forum at www.DarwinAwards.com/forum fosters rich communication and debate. In the course of its evolution from fireside gathering to library commons, guidelines were agreed upon to help people get the most out of their stay. I share this Forum Decorum document as a public service to discussion boards everywhere.

- *Respect your privacy.*
  It is friendly to have a public email address so people can contact you privately offline, but it's no fun to find a weirdo on your doorstep. Be sensible! Protect yourself with an anonymous email address.
- *Entertainment is provided by you.*
  This is a place to have fun, so relax and pull up a barstool. We're a friendly crowd and we don't mind laughing at ourselves and each other. We are even amused when we're caught taking ourselves too seriously, as we do in this document.
- *Obey Godwin's Law.*
  See Appendix 4: Godwin's Law, page 221.
- *Be polite.*
  As with all human interactions,
  courtesy is always welcome
  and surprisingly effective.
- *DON'T TYPE YOUR WHOLE MESSAGE IN UPPERCASE.*
  It's difficult to read and feels like you're shouting. A short stretch of uppercase is SUFFICIENT to emphasize a point. Also try to use capitals and punctuation.

- *Pay attention to yer grammer and spellings.*
  It's all about communication, and poorly constructed messages are confusing. If your words are important enough to write, they're important enough to write well. Give our brains an idea to chew on, not a cryptogram.
- *Forgive the spelling and grammar mistakes of others.*
  Not everyone types easily, learned English at home, or has decades of practice.
- *Re-read before posting and reflect* on your own reaction if you were to receive this message from another poster. Convincing? Hostile? Rambling? Time spent making a message clearer and more persuasive is always time well spent.
- *Grammar police sometimes strike without warning!*
  — Break your message into logical paragraphs.
  — Restrict your sentences to sensible lengths.
  — Don't double-space short sentences to fill space.
  — Etc.
- *Avoid public flames sent in anger.*
  If you must flame, do so after you've cooled down a bit and can make your flame constructive. Messages sent in the heat of the moment usually exacerbate a situation, and are oft regretted later. If what you have to say is hurtful, ask yourself why you need to hurt someone, and consider a private email instead.

Apply "Happy Quotes" as needed!
www.DarwinAwards.com/book/okay.html

- *Pointed humor* is perceived as sarcasm. If you're not being sarcastic, say so. Maybe you are being sarcastic without knowing it.
- *Forums have the immediacy of a conversation* but are devoid of body language. The Internet has evolved *emoticons* as an answer to this lack of shrugs and grimaces. There are hundreds of them, some more common than others, all used to convey nuances and make your messages clearer. Use them sparingly or they won't be very effective.
- *Mind your manners.*
  Make sure you are familiar with a thread before tossing in your thoughts. In general, keep to the subject as much as possible, with the occasional brief detour. If you want to branch off onto a tangent, it's a good idea to start a new thread.
- *If you make a request, don't forget to say please.*
  If someone helps you, it doesn't hurt to say thank you. This might sound trivial, but people often forget their real-world manners at the door (or Internet portal). It's astonishing how much these familiar courtesies will help you persuade others to your side.
- *Don't expect an immediate answer.*
  The lack of a quick response does not mean anyone is ignoring you. People check into forums on a random basis and have limited time. On the other hand, if nobody responds at all, probably everyone either agrees or isn't interested in that particular conversational gambit. It happens to everyone and is no cause for offense. Try another topic.

ADVICE FROM PHILOSOPHY FORUM MEMBERS

SLEEPLESS
Be yourself, speak honestly and truthfully, listen and think, and all will be well.

RANGERMOM
Don't tell people they are ignorant, uneducated oafs, stupid, fearful of knowledge, etc., just because they have a different point of view. *Most* people have reason for their beliefs that require thought and examination of many aspects. Respect them for that, even if you disagree.

CERBERUS
Do some homework before you go spouting off on a topic. Read the whole thread before posting something new. Don't take anything personally. Don't post for posting's sake.

KIKOV
Wear your flames with pride, then jump right back in. If you become a totally offensive jerk, someone will let you know. It's okay to reevaluate your position. Then let us know why you changed your mind. We seriously want to know.

DEV
Share your opinion, post controversial topics, talk about religion and politics and all the things Mom told you not to discuss at the dinner table.

COMMON SENSE CAUTION

Do not change anything in real life based on Internet personal interactions. It is okay to disagree with others, to make a mistake, to lose face. We have our own viewpoints and our own personality quirks. But I have known people to quit jobs and leave fraternal orders based on perceived failures in online social interactions. It's not worth it!

If you embarrass yourself, you will live through it and your interactions will grow richer. Others will respect you for your honesty. And as a last resort you can always create a new pseudonym.

Read the history of the Philosophy Forum:
www.darwinawards.com/book/history.html

4. Godwin's Law

GODWIN'S LAW:

The longer a Usenet discussion becomes, the more likely it is to disintegrate into a flame involving a comparison with Nazis or Hitler. As the thread ages, the probability approaches one.

There is a tradition in many groups that, once this occurs, that thread is over, and whoever mentioned the Nazis has automatically lost whatever argument was in progress. This is known as Godwin's Law.

Godwin's Law guarantees the existence of an upper bound on thread length. There is a widely held codicil that any intentional triggering of Godwin's Law in order to invoke its thread-ending effects will be unsuccessful.

More about Godwin's Law:
www.DarwinAwards.com/book/godwin.html

Story Index

A Fell Death (*DA*) 95
A Medieval Tale (*PA*) 139
Aircraft Airhead (*HM*) 35
airplane 35
Alaska 63, 121
Alberta, Canada 92
Albuquerque, New Mexico 69
alcohol 21, 39, 48, 55, 69, 74, 76, 93, 181, 200, 205, 210
All Aboard (*HM*) 53
amateur electrician 61, 68
Amsterdam, Netherlands 18
anesthetic 14, 169
Anchorage, Alaska 121
aqueduct 105
Archery Practice (*HM*) 99
Arizona 118, 193
Arkansas 135, 204
arson 29
Australia 53, 55, 65, 74, 93, 159
Author Biography (*Appendix*) 215
automobile 16, 32, 33, 34, 36, 38, 41, 46, 67, 69, 81, 93, 193
avalanche 63
Avignon, France 105
Baden-Würtemberg, Germany 15
Baker, David L., personal account 136
balloons, weather 200
Baltimore, Maryland 181
bar brawl 92
bathtub 49
beans 53, 199
bear 40, 121

bed sheet, used as rope 155
beer 55, 74, 76, 164, 181, 200, 205, 210
Bern, Switzerland 178
bicycle 174
Binky the Bear 121
boat, capsized 47
boat, sailboat 53
boat, speedboat 47
boat, yacht 53
Bodacious Bud (*HM*) 165
Body Canyoning (*Not a Darwin*) 178
bomb, homemade 20
bomb, letter 16
bomb, nuclear 145
bonfire construction 176
bow and arrow 99
bra, underwire 175
Brandenburg, Germany 19
Brewery Mishap (*UL*) 55
bricklayer 103
Brisbane, Australia 159
broccoli 152
Brush with Stupidity (*PA*) 41
Buchman, Jim, personal account 105
bullet, use as fuse 204
Bulletproof? (*DA*) 89
Burger King 29
cabbage 199
Cactus Tales (*UL*) 118
Cairo, Egypt 48, 116
Calgary, Canada 92
California 49, 136, 154, 161, 166, 200, 203, 208
Call Girl (*HM*) 164
Cambodia 114
camera 15, 30, 40

Canada 32, 38, 92, 98, 99, 158, 186
cannon, wooden 139
car chase, low-speed 166
Car Safety (*Discussion*) 58
carbon dioxide gas 55, 180
catheter 107
cavern 17
Ceres, California 203
chairs, collapsing 77
champagne 105
Charleston, Illinois 71
Cheez Whiz (*HM*) 96
Chicago, Illinois 158
chicken 198
Chicken with a Train (*HM*) 101
Chihuahua, Mexico 17
chili pepper 22
choking hazard 163
Christians, unusual sect 33, 49
Christmas Tree (*DA*) 32
cigar 141
cigarette 37, 143
Circular Reasoning (*DA*) 70
City Living (*Discussion*) 150
Civilization Memes (*Discussion*) 26
Clearwater, Florida 81
cliff, leaping from 52
cliff, wreckage on 193
cocaine 152, 158
Coke machine 195
Colorado 61
Columbus, Ohio 87
compulsive collector syndrome 186
computer hacker 167
condoms 53

confession 159
Connecticut..39
construction worker 61, 70, 100
Cooley, Don, personal account 23
Coors Light and the UltraLight (*HM*) 76
copper, theft of 156
copy machine, bogus 159
copying, an iceberg sport 182
Count Your Chickens (*DA*) 198
counterfeit money 152
Croatia 131
Crystal Daze (*DA*) 17
crystals, selenite 17
dare, taking a 114, 133
Darwin's Theory of Evolution (*Introduction*) 6
death, automobile 16, 32, 67, 193, 205
death, bee sting 114
death, burnt to 19
death, by choking 115
death, by dragging 73, 74
death, by hanging 65, 91
death, by lightning 175
death, by liposuction 14
death, by methanol 21
death, concussion 36
death, crushed to 17, 95, 176, 195, 205
death, decapitation 80, 132
death, dehydration 186
death, drowning 33, 34, 46, 47, 48, 52, 52, 55, 174, 178, 198
death, drowning upon impact 50, 51
death, electrocution 61, 66, 68, 156
death, from friendly fire 89
death, from hiccups 181
death, from hypothermia 29, 63, 152, 182
death, from thumbtack 184

death, gunshot .71, 87, 90, 116, 134, 196, 197

death, in bathtub 49

death, in explosion 16, 20, 129, 131, 132, 133

death, in forklift 65

death, on scooter 69

death, overdose 158

death, stabbing 159

death, suffocation 88, 199

death, trampling 30

death, upon impact 15, 18, 31, 48, 92, 93, 93, 94, 154, 155, 208

decompression 208

Denmark 37

Denver, Colorado 61

Des Moines, Iowa 91

desert, as racetrack 193

desert, collecting plants in 118

desert, sleeping in 116

diesel fuel 141

Dive to Death (*DA*) 50

diving, Scuba 208

divorce, bitter 19

Do Bikes Float? (*Not a Darwin*) 174

Do It Yourself, Do Yourself In (*DA*) 61

Dodging Drink Dues (*DA*) 48

dog 117, 135, 137, 210

Dog and Jeep (*UL*) 210

Doggone Foot (*HM*) 117

Dogs and Darwinism (*Discussion*) 110

dolphins, impersonating 122

drowning 178, 198

drowning, in beer 55

drowning, in car 34

drowning, while bathing 49

drowning, while boating 47

drowning, while diving 50

drowning, while fishing 46, 52
drowning, while jumping 51
drowning, while saving money 48
drowning, while showing off 52
duck hunting 210
duct tape 29
Duct Tape (DA) 47
Dumb Drunk (HM) 39
Dunedin, New Zealand 31
dynamite 210
Eat the Young (PA) 40
Egypt 48, 116, 198
Electrifying Stunt (DA) 66
electrocution 61, 66, 75, 156, 175
elephant, trampled by 30
Emergency Locating Transmitter 162
emergency room 23, 107, 123
Emergency Room Excitement (PA) 23
England 21, 51, 52, 54, 68, 70, 88, 96, 162, 167, 175
Enraged Elephant (DA) 30
Escaping Conviction (DA) 155
Ethanol Schmethanol (DA) 21
executioners, playful 65
explosion, air mattress 180
explosion, averted 145
explosion, cannon 139
explosion, dynamite 210
explosion, grenade 131
explosion, lighter fluid 37
explosion, solvent 203
explosion, tire 129
explosion, triggered by gunfire 133
Explosive Mix of Girls (HM) 37
Fairbanks, Alaska 63
Fantastic Plastic Lover (DA) 88

Fast Food Fatality (DA) 29
Fatal Case of Hiccups (Not a Darwin) 181
Fatal Footwear Fashion (DA) 36
FBI and bank robbers 171
FBIP 107
feces 54, 102, 166
Feeding the Dolphins (PA) 122
fellatio 123
Ferguson 2, Thieves 0 (HM) 162
Fifteen Minutes of Flame (UL) 137
fire engine 81
fire, airplane 136
fire, bonfire 176
fire, forest 208
fire, house 19, 135, 137
fire, lawnmower 143
firecracker 77
Fireworks Fiasco (DA) 132
first-degree burn, defined 75
Fish Gag (DA) 115
fish, killer 115
fisherman, avid 47, 52
fishermen, avid 46
Fishing with No Compass (DA) 46
Flames of Passion (DA) 19
flare, road 141
flatulence 199
Florida 34, 81, 92, 100, 117, 122
food, overindulgence 22
Forklift Safety Video (DA) 65
Forum Decorum (Appendix) 216
Fourth of July 50, 132
fourth-degree burn, defined 75
France 105
Frog Giggin' Accident (UL) 204

fugitives, befuddled 161
gallows 65
gardener 61, 165
gasoline 135, 136, 143
gasoline, theft gone wrong 166
genitals, severed 160
geode 17
Georgia 129
Germany 15, 19, 186
Ghana 89
Glasgow, Scotland 156
God 33, 49
God Saves? (*DA*) 91
Godwin's Law (*Appendix*) 221
gopher 203
Grenade Juggler (*DA*) 131
Guinness Book of World Records 22, 31
Guitars 'n' Guns (*DA*) 134
gun 71, 87, 89, 90, 92, 116, 117, 133, 134, 167, 196, 197, 210
gunshot, protection from 89
gunshot, self-inflicted 90
gunshot, to testicle 204
Guyana, South America 35
hair dryer 41
hanging, accidental 65
Hardheads (*DA*) 93
Hastings, New Zealand 163
helium gas 200
Herndon, William D., personal account 79
heroin 158
hiccups, fatal 181
highmarking, snow sport 63
homemade bomb 20
homemade lie detector 159
Hornet Challenge (*DA*) 114

Horsing Around (*PA*) 123
House Hunting Gone Awry (*HM*) 75
Houston, Texas 50
Human Popsicle (*DA*) 152
Hungary 139
Huntingdon Valley, Pennsylvania 102
husband, cuckolded 20
Hyde Park, London 175
hypothermia 38, 63, 152
ice 38, 46, 182, 210
Ice Floe Frolic (*Not a Darwin*) 182
Idaho 23
Illinois 33, 71, 160
Indiana 29, 76, 165
Instant Sunrise (*PA*) 145
insurance claim 103, 210
Intelligent Design Theory (*Discussion*) 126
Intersecting Darwins (*DA*) 67
Iowa 91
jail, escaping 155
janitors 203
Japan 36
JATO (*DA*) 193
Jeep Grand Cherokee 210
Jesus, following in His footsteps 49
Jones, Jocko, personal account 143
juggling grenades 131
jump, from bridge 51
jump, from cliff 52
Junk Food Junkie (*DA*) 195
Just Say No! (*DA*) 158
Kaboom! (*HM*) 135
Kansas 152
ketamine, anesthetic 169
keys, missing 102

Khabarovsk, Russia 20
Killing Time (DA) 156
Kismet, Karma, Destiny (Discussion) 12
knife 35, 159, 205
La Paz, Mexico 90
laboratory accident 21
Lafayette, Indiana 76
Lake Erie 46
lake, frozen 210
lake, Summit Lake 63
Latin America 77
lawnchair 137
Lawnchair Larry (HM) 200
lawnmower 143
left shoe, found in wreckage 76
Legaspi, Philippines 22
Leone, Gene, personal account 40
lidocaine, anesthetic 14
lie detector, homemade 159
life jacket, ill-fitting 47
lighter fluid 37
lighter, cigarette 37, 41, 135
lightning 175
Liposuction Tragedy (DA) 14
literary agent, clueless 137
Little Rock, Arkansas 135
Liverpool, England 162
Lobster Vasectomy (UL) 124
London, England 70, 175
Los Angeles, California 152, 165, 200
lottery 161
Louisiana 167
lumberjack, erstwhile 95
Mad Trombonist (UL) 77
mail, returned 16

Malaysia .... .65
Mammoth Mountain, California 154
Man and Cactus (PA) 142
Man with Gas Can (PA) 143
Mania Strikes Back (Not a Darwin) 186
marijuana 107, 152, 165
Martin, Gerald, personal account 122
Maryland 181
mechanic...129, 143
Medical Misadventures (PA) 169
Melancon, Sarah and Paul, personal account 41
Melbourne, Australia.....................................55
Memphis, Tennessee 67
Men Eating Chili (HM) 22
Metallica Concert Misadventure (UL) 205
methane gas 199
methane gas, human 199
methanol 21
Mexico 17, 90
Michigan 66, 145, 210
Middle East 16
Midnight Special (DA) 196
Mineola, New York 14
Miracle Mile (PA) 81
Mongrel Mob 163
Montezuma, Georgia 129
Morsel of Evidence (HM) 163
Moscow Marauder (DA) 20
motor home 166
Netherlands, Amsterdam 18
New Dating Technique (DA) 90
New Hampshire 184
New Mexico 69
New York 132, 137
New York, Mineola 14

New Zealand 31, 163
Newfoundland, Canada 182
Newton, North Carolina 196
nicotine urge 37, 203
noose 65, 91
North Carolina 196
Norwich, England 51
nuclear device 145
nudity 15
Ocean, Atlantic 52, 174, 182
Ocean, Pacific 208
Ohio 46, 87, 101, 123, 152, 162
Online Safety (*Discussion*) 84
Ontario, Canada 38
orchestra 77
Oregon 47
Our Brightest Cheerleaders (*Not a Darwin*) 180
Out with a Bang! (*DA*) 129
overdose, lidocaine 14
overdose, veterinary drug 169
Oxford University 21
oxyacetylene gas 180
Paks, Hungary 139
Passionate Plunge (*DA*) 51
penis injury 107, 123
Pennsylvania 95, 102, 155, 159
Perilous Pose (*DA*) 15
Perth, Australia 65
Petrillo, Alan, personal account 81
Philippines 22
Phnom Penh, Cambodia 114
photocopier, imaginary 159
pilot, attacked 35
pilot, inept 76
pilot, oblivious 208

pilot, would-be 200
Pittsburgh, Pennsylvania 155
Plane Stupid (HM) 136
Planning Ahead (HM) 167
Polar Bear Lesson (PA) 121
Polgar, Tamas, personal account 139
police officer, dead 158
police officer, innovative 159
Pont de Garde, France 105
pool, shallow 50
porcupine quills 23
Port St. John, Florida 117
Pouch Cove, Newfoundland 182
Power Punch Proves Fatal (DA) 68
power windows, danger of 34
prisoner, escape of 155
professor, absent-minded 21
Prop Arc Safety (PA) 80
punch, well-meaning 181
punching bag 68
pyrospectacular 132
Quebec, Canada 32
Radnor, Pennsylvania 159
railroad car 141
railroad crossing 67
railroad timetable 156
rapist, career-ending injury 160
rapist, gullible 164
Rappin' on Heaven's Door (DA) 87
Renton, Washington 197
rescue, by children 52, 102, 182
rescue, by Leatherman tool 161
rescue, by U.S. Coast Guard 47, 122
rescue, from balloon lawnchair 200
rescue, from landfill 98

rescue, of trees 32
Revenge of the Gopher (*HM*) 203
revenge, apt 160
revenge, by explosion 20
revenge, by fire 19
revenge, danger of seeking 159
revenge, midair 35
revenge, of a ski lift tower 154
river, Chungu River 115
river, Columbia River 47
river, Nile River . . . : 48
river, Saxteen River 178
river, Wensum River 51
road flare 141
Robot Reaper (*PA*) 79
rocket, JATO 193
roof . . . . : 18
Rothenburg, Germany 15
Ruaha National Park, Tanzania 30
Rubbish! (*DA*) 31
Rules and Eligibility (*Intro*) 3
Russian roulette 71, 87, 90, 134
safari encounter 30
safety harness 70, 100
saguaro cactus 118
Sand Surfing (*DA*) 74
Saskatchewan, Canada 98
Scooter Snuff (*DA*) 69
Scotland 156
Scuba Divers and Forest Fires (*UL*) 208
seat belt, omitting 65
Seattle, Washington 94, 166
second-degree burn, defined 75
security guard 71, 136
Settle the Score (*DA*) 92

sewage, raw 54, 166
Sewer Shower (*HM*) 54
sex, odd request 88
sex, with rodent 23
sharks 122
shatterproof glass 155
Sheep Sleep (*DA*) 116
Shell Shot (*DA*) 133
Shepparton, Australia 74
shoes, platform 36
Shotgun Pepsi (*Not a Darwin*) 184
Show Off (*DA*) 52
Sidi Barrani, Egypt 116
Sigma Pseudo™ Corpse Scent 188
Siphon! (*HM*) 166
siphoning gas 136
ski run, asphalt 31
Ski Theft Backfires (*DA*) 154
skiing, behind truck 74
skiing, on stolen property 154
sleep, near sheep 116
sleep, on roof 18
sleep, while driving 34
Sleepfalling (*DA*) 18
Slovenia 52
snow 38, 95
Snow Bunnies (*HM*) 38
snowball fight 73
Snowball's Chance in Hell (*DA*) 73
snowmobile 63
soap, slippery 49
sobriety test 39
Sobriety Test (*HM*) 168
soccer player, defensive 162
solvent 203

South Africa 48
South America 35
South Carolina 93
Speciation (Discussion) 190
spider, tarantula 118
St. Petersburg, Florida 100
Stab in the Dark (DA) 159
stalactite 17
sterilization 124, 160, 204
student, university 31, 101, 131, 176
Styrofoam and gasoline 143
Surviving Stupidity (Introduction) 8
Sweet Release (DA) 71
swimming pool 50
Switzerland 178
Tangmere, England 54
Tanzania 30
tarantula nesting habits 118
teenagers 37, 121, 179, 182
telephone, cell phone 34, 164
telephone, fateful call 39, 165, 196
Tennessee 67
tequila 69
terrorist 16
testicles, and rusty spoon 176
testicles, injured 92, 124, 204
testicles, turned over to police 160
Testing Faith (DA) 33
Texas 50, 133, 176
Texas A&M Bonfire (Not a Darwin) 176
Thanksgiving 176
That Sinking Feeling (DA) 34
The Bricklayer (UL) 103
The Last Supper (DA) 199
The Sting (HM) 161

Thickstun, Tyler, personal account 121
thief, bank 167, 171
thief, Burger King 29
thief, church 91
thief, copper 156
thief, drug 158, 163, 169
thief, foam pad 154
thief, fuel 136, 166
thief, homing device 162
thief, inept 158, 167, 197
thief, lobster 124
thief, misguided 162
thief, steamroller 165
third-degree burn, defined 75
Throwing Stones (*DA*) 16
Tied to His Work (*HM*) 100
timber, falling 95
tire repair 129
Toilet Trap (*HM*) 102
Tokyo, Japan 36
toll collectors 73
tomatoes, role in death 61
Toronto, Canada 99
tourist 30, 105
Tourist Trap (*PA*) 105
traffic, standing amid 33
trailer park 135, 159
train 67, 101, 156
trash can 31
Trash Compactor (*HM*) 98
trombone 77
truck, atop corpse 205
truck, dragged by 73
truck, missing 152
truck, needing repair 204

truck, riding atop 93
truck, surfing behind 74
truck, towing nuclear device 145
Tube Snake (*PA*) 107
Two Avalanche Alaskan (*DA*) 63
UltraLight aircraft 76
Underwire Bras Deadly (*Not a Darwin*) 175
United States, Alaska 63, 121
United States, Arizona 118, 193
United States, Arkansas 135, 204
United States, California 49, 136, 154, 161, 166, 200, 203, 208
United States, Colorado 61
United States, Connecticut 39
United States, Florida 34, 81, 92, 100, 117, 122
United States, Georgia 129
United States, Idaho 23
United States, Illinois 33, 71, 160
United States, Indiana 29, 76, 165
United States, Iowa 91
United States, Kansas 152
United States, Louisiana 167
United States, Maryland 181
United States, Mexico 69
United States, Michigan 66, 145, 210
United States, New Hampshire 184
United States, New York 14, 132, 137
United States, North Carolina 196
United States, Ohio 46, 87, 101, 123, 152, 162
United States, Oregon 47
United States, Pennsylvania 95, 102, 155, 159
United States, South Carolina 93
United States, Tennessee 67
United States, Texas 50, 133, 176
United States, Virginia 141
United States, Washington 94, 166, 197, 205

United States, West Virginia 143
United States, Wyoming 40
urethra, abused 107
Ur-inate-iot (*DA*) 94
urine 94, 102
U.S. Air Force 145, 193, 200
U.S. Coast Guard 47, 122
U.S. Navy 80
vacuum 14, 88
Vanderholm, J.S., personal account 169
veterinarian 169
video, rap 87
video, safety 65
Virginia 141
Walking on Water (*DA*) 49
warehouse, automated 79
Washington 94, 166, 197, 205
weather balloons 200
Website Biography (*Appendix*) 213
Weed Seeds and Biodiversity (*Discussion*) 44
Weedwacker wire 107
well, and chicken 198
West Virginia 143
What Are They? (*Introduction*) 2
Where Do Darwins Come From? (*Introduction*) 9
Wichita, Kansas 152
witchcraft 89
Workin' on the Railroad (*PA*) 141
Wrong Time, Wrong Place (*DA*) 197
Wyoming 40
Yellowstone National Park 40
You Said a Mouthful (*DA*) 160
Zambia 115
zoo 30